First published in Great Britain in 2018 by

Bristol University Press
University of Bristol
1-9 Old Park Hill
Bristol
BS2 8BB
UK
t: +44 (0)117 954 5940
www.bristoluniversitypress.co.uk

North America office:
Bristol University Press
c/o The University of Chicago Press
1427 East 60th Street
Chicago, IL 60637, USA
t: +1 773 702 7700
f: +1 773 702 9756
sales@press.uchicago.edu
www.press.uchicago.edu

British Library Cataloguing in Publication Data
A catalogue record for this book is available from the British Library.

Library of Congress Cataloging-in-Publication Data
A catalog record for this book has been requested.

ISBN 978-1-5292-0358-5 (hardback)
ISBN 978-1-5292-0366-0 (ePub)
ISBN 978-1-5292-0368-4 (Mobi)
ISBN 978-1-5292-0361-5 (ePDF)

Cover design by blu inc, Bristol
Front cover: image kindly supplied by Shutterstock
Printed and bound in Great Britain by CPI Group (UK) Ltd, Croydon, CR0 4YY
Bristol University Press uses environmentally responsible print partners

FSC
www.fsc.org
MIX
Paper from responsible sources
FSC® C013604

Dedication

With good reason, books such as this are conventionally dedicated to those who have died in prison. However, this practice can inadvertently shape a sense that such events are safely in the past. Although the deaths I describe are in the past, sadly their circumstances are *now* not then. The bereavements are not over for the families left behind. Incredibly sick people still languish in prison. These are live issues.

I therefore dedicate this book to those prisoners who are suicidal in prisons around the world *now*, and to their families.

Contents

Detailed contents

Acronyms

ACCT	Assessment, Care in Custody, Teamwork
CPS	Crown Prosecution Service
EHRC	Equalities and Human Rights Commission
HMIP	Her Majesty's Inspectorate of Prisons
HMP	Her Majesty's Prison
HMPPS	Her Majesty's Prison and Probation Service
HMYOI	Her Majesty's Young Offender Institution
HSE	Health and Safety Executive
IMB	Independent Monitoring Board
MoJ	Ministry of Justice
NAO	National Audit Office
NOMS	National Offender Management Service
NPM	National Preventative Mechanism
PFD	Coroners' Reports to Prevent Future Deaths
PPO	Prison and Probation Ombudsman
WHO	World Health Organization
YOI	Young Offender Institution

Notes on the author

Dr Philippa Tomczak is a Senior Research Fellow at the University of Nottingham. She held a Leverhulme Trust Early Career Fellowship at the University of Sheffield Centre for Criminological Research from 2015 to 2018. In 2017 she was awarded a British Academy Rising Star Engagement Award to coordinate CRIMVOL: the new international, multidisciplinary criminal justice voluntary sector research network for academics, practitioners and policy makers. She researches punishment and criminal justice, particularly prison suicide and the criminal justice voluntary sector.

Philippa undertook her BA and MSc at the University of Oxford (England), and her PhD at the University of Manchester (England). Philippa's first monograph, *The Penal Voluntary Sector*, won the 2017 British Society of Criminology Book Prize and received impressive reviews. Philippa welcomes opportunities to present and discuss her work with others.

Acknowledgements

I am extremely grateful for generous financial support from the Leverhulme Trust Early Career Fellowship and the University of Sheffield Centre for Criminological Research, for enabling me to produce this book and the research upon which it is based. I have benefited enormously through expert mentoring from Professor Joanna Shapland whilst at Sheffield.

1

Prison suicide and its aftermath

Introduction

Prison suicide is a global problem. Suicide is 'often the single most common cause of death in correctional settings' (World Health Organization (WHO), 2007: 1). National rates of prisoner suicide are consistently several times higher than rates in the general population (Fazel et al, 2017). Imprisonment is recognised as a stressor that can trigger suicidal behaviour (Larney and Farrell, 2017) and even induce psychological disturbance amongst prisoners with no prior disorder (Liebling, 2007: 433). Given that there are now 10.35 million people in prison globally (Coyle et al, 2016), this is worrying. 'The need to monitor what goes on in prisons is more important and urgent than ever' (Seddon, 2010: 278), not least because all those in a malfunctioning system kick downwards, so the detainee suffers most (Carver and Handley, 2016: 633).

Prisons, along with closed institutions of all kinds, pose accountability challenges for democratic societies (Harding, 2007). Suicides in closed penal institutions with coercive powers over detainees leave prisons open to legal challenges and threaten the right to life, which is 'the most fundamental of all human rights, the basic pre-condition of the enjoyment of other rights' (Owen and Macdonald, 2015: 121). Suicides often affect fellow prisoners and custodial staff (Sweeney et al, 2018) and may be particularly traumatic bereavements for prisoners' families and friends because of the exceptional and often controversial circumstances (Liebling, 2007). Prison suicides are also economically problematic, draining England and Wales' public purse of up to £385 million in 2016.[1] However, the stark reality is that 'many (suicides) could have been prevented if risks had been properly recognised and addressed' (Owen and Macdonald, 2015: 309). Prison suicide is thus a *substantially* (although not entirely) *preventable crisis*[2] with significant human and economic impacts. Between April 2012 and March 2013, prisoners in England and Wales were more likely to take their own lives than construction employees were to be killed at work (Doyle and McGrath, 2016: 159). Nevertheless, 'dying in jail, which ... occurs with admitted regularity, has been largely overlooked by social scientists' (Liebling, 1992: 23). The USA has very recently had growing interest, but 'death in prison in the UK is presented to be a rare phenomenon, for those few who serve whole life tariffs and those who die unexpectedly/ unpredictably during their term of imprisonment'[3] (Girling and Seal, 2016: 271).

1 England and Wales' *95* prison suicides in the 12 months to September 2015 were estimated to cost at least £160m and up to *£300m*' (Howard League, 2016a: 1). In the 12 months to December 2016, there were *122* self-inflicted deaths in prison custody (Ministry of Justice (MoJ), 2017: 1).

2 Prisoners, having the same rights as non-prisoners excepting freedom of movement, have the right to die and may hold a sustained and settled desire to end their lives (Pridmore and Pridmore, 2017). Suicide prevention requires limits. Australian scholarship recognises the very fine line between preventive interventions, such as using 'wet cells' for the 'care and protection' of vulnerable suicidal prisoners, and inflicting a humiliating, cruel procedure to prevent suicide at any cost. 'Wet cells' are equipped with a tear-proof canvas tunic instead of clothes, a canvas blanket and mattress on the floor. They have clear Perspex walls for observation from a distance; a television screen visible to the prisoner through the wall for stimulation; a horizontal, two-inch line painted around the walls above the floor for visual orientation; and a toilet bowl and washbasin (Bell, 1999; see also Cliquennois and Champetier, 2013).

3 There has been some policy and practice attention. The Chief Inspector of Prisons published 'Suicide is Everyone's Concern' in 1999. The

Research has sought to examine the relative contribution of prison and prisoner characteristics to suicide incidence.[4] For example, suicide has been found to increase as levels of purposeful activity decrease across prison categories (Leese et al, 2006). The importance of prison staff perceptions and attitudes to suicide attempts has been highlighted (Liebling, 1992). The role of overcrowding, as both a stressor and a protective factor, has been explored (Fazel et al, 2017; van Ginneken et al, 2017). Many have considered prisoners' imported vulnerabilities, such as those relating to mental health and drug use (Liebling, 1992; Rivlin et al, 2013; Walker and Towl, 2016), and noted that custodial sentences and remand are disproportionately directed at disadvantaged and vulnerable populations (Liebling, 2007: 442). These valuable studies have established that prison suicide prevention should address complex interactions between individual and systemic risk factors[5] (Bartlett et al, 2018; Stoliker, 2018). However, the investigatory processes occurring *after* prison suicides have largely escaped attention. Investigations can be undertaken by internal Prison Service investigators, police, ombudsmen and coroners, for example. This book explores key questions, including: how do these investigations operate? How are they experienced by stakeholders? What do they achieve? Are they any more than legitimising functions that shore up state power?[6] Adopting a post-death vantage point

Parliamentary Joint Committee on Human Rights published reports on 'Deaths in Custody' in 2004 and an interim report on 'Mental Health and Deaths in Prison' in 2017.

4 Use of police force during arrest has also been correlated with greater incidence of manic and depressive symptoms amongst prisoners (Meade et al, 2017).

5 Individual imported risk factors and prison-induced distress seem to play different roles in different types of prison suicide (Liebling and Ludlow, 2016: 226).

6 Regarding Canada, Razack (2015: 31) states that 'inquests and inquiries have mapped indifference and abandonment in the same ways for 150 years'.

is also useful to better illuminate the vicious cycles that often spiral from suicides and have knock-on implications in future prison incidents. These vicious cycles are underappreciated in scholarship, policy and practice but provide a strong rationale for prison suicide prevention work.

This chapter explains the research underpinning this book and contextualises prison suicide by (i) defining prison suicide and problematising its definition, highlighting implications for the practical management of prison suicide; (ii) illustrating how prison suicides can trigger suicidogenic vicious cycles and considering the potential roles of institutional apathy and prisoner stigma in suicide prevention work; (iii) providing a brief overview of recent Safer Custody developments; and (iv) describing the structure of this book.

Globally, the post-death vantage point has not received adequate attention in scholarship or practice:[7] 'it is a widely overlooked problem that in many prisons deaths are frequent and most of them are considered "normal" or "natural" and not necessarily investigated while some of them were preventable' (Gaggioli and Elger, 2017: 35). The WHO's influential guide 'Preventing Suicides in Jails and Prisons' (2007: 20–21) devotes just a single side to 'If a suicide occurs', despite recognising the increased risk of further suicide attempts for four weeks after a death; the potential for prison staff to experience feelings including anger, resentment, guilt and sadness; the need to officially document and report the death; and the importance of 'providing the constructive feedback necessary to improve future suicide prevention'. Bollman et al (2017) identify national variability in investigations (or lack thereof) into detention deaths

Burton and Carlen (1979: 48) argue that 'inquiries into particular crises is to represent failure as temporary, or no failure at all, and to re-establish the image of administrative and legal coherence and rationality'.

7 Razack (2015) provides a particular racialised account of inquests and inquiries into Indigenous deaths in Canadian custody.

and provide a practical guide for the short-term aftermath, including recommended procedures for scene management, evidence collection, management of the body, informing the next of kin and post-mortem examination. Wangmo et al (2014: 31) rightly emphasise that 'it is important that thorough investigation of death in custody is performed' but focus again on short-term forensic investigations, noting (Wangmo et al, 2014: 36) the 'urgent need to systematically collect standardised data in many countries' from autopsies and laboratory analysis. Although some jurisdictions have yet to implement such short-term investigations, a growing body of jurisdictions have established additional, longer-term interrelated investigatory processes following prison suicides.

Article 2 (the right to life) of the European Convention on Human Rights, to which all 47 Council of Europe Member States are party, obliges states to investigate deaths of those involuntarily in custody (Mowbray, 2002). Article 2 is explored in detail in Chapter Two. Furthermore, the Optional Protocol to the United Nations Convention against Torture[8] now has 87 states party, all of which are required by Article 17 to establish a National Preventative Mechanism (NPM). NPMs comprise bodies that regularly examine conditions of detention and treatment of detainees, make recommendations, and comment on legislation with the aim of improving treatment and conditions in detention.[9] Sixty-six states have a designated NPM at the time of writing.[10] NPMs take different forms in different states (Steinerte, 2014; Lappi-Seppälä and Koskenniemi, 2017). Sharing the lessons from deaths in custody and their implications

8 Optional Protocol to the Convention against Torture and other Cruel, Inhuman or Degrading Treatment or Punishment. Adopted December 2002, into force on June 2006.

9 https://s3-eu-west-2.amazonaws.com/npm-prod-storage-19n0nag2nk8xk/uploads/2018/02/6.4122_NPM_AR2016-17_v4_web.pdf.

10 www.apt.ch/en/opcat-database/.

for detention monitoring and inspection is a key task for the UK's NPM.[11]

Given the provisions of Article 2 and the Optional Protocol, and further international jurisprudence and soft laws recognising the fundamental human rights to life and to be treated humanely in detention (Wangmo et al, 2014: 31), the lack of attention to post-prison suicide investigations is peculiar and problematic. Opportunities to learn lessons and save lives could be being squandered, given that 'deaths in custody represent the extreme end of a continuum of near deaths and injuries. … A proactive post-inquest strategy in response to verdicts and reports can not only avert deaths but also risks to custodial health and safety generally' (Coles and Shaw, 2012: 2; see also Gaggioli and Elger, 2017: 47). The airline industry has demonstrated how post-incident investigations and lesson-learning programmes can be effective. For example, the fatality risk for commercial aviation in the United States declined by 83% between 1998 and 2008, largely because of investigations into accidents and smaller incidents (Madsen et al, 2016). The Federal Aviation Administration runs voluntary disclosure programmes which generate important secondary learning, beyond information about violations (Mills and Reiss, 2014). In criminal justice, however, near misses generate 'grim sighs of relief, but little incentive for instigating an analysis' (Doyle, 2010: 135). In light of the substantial socioeconomic costs and harms of prison suicide, and evidence that post-incident investigations can be valuable, this book addresses an important gap in knowledge that deserves sustained attention and has many potential implications for practice. Prison suicides and post-death investigations are issues of global importance, and this book provides a case study of the investigations following prison suicides in England and Wales. This case study has relevance across jurisdictions, be they

[11] www.crimeandjustice.org.uk/sites/crimeandjustice.org.uk/files/FINAL%20CCJS_Briefing17_Dec15.pdf.

primarily concerned with implementing short-term prison death investigations, meeting the requirements of Article 2, or developing and refining their NPM. It is nevertheless important to apply this case study beyond England and Wales with attention to varying penal cultures and conditions (for example, Pratt and Eriksson, 2013), and each jurisdiction's geopolitical, sociocultural and legal intricacies (for example, Steinerte, 2014).

The case study: England and Wales

Prisons in England and Wales provide a useful case study, having 'a large range of regulatory[12] institutions that may serve as comparators for regulation elsewhere' (van Zyl Smit, 2010: 509). Furthermore, England and Wales' Inspectorate of Prisons, which coordinates the UK's NPM, is well established, has a 'track record of principle-driven and independent external regulation' (van Zyl Smit, 2010: 555–556) and 'pervasive' influence that has contributed to improving prison conditions (van Zyl Smit, 2010: 532; see also Carver, 2016: 136–140). Nevertheless, prison suicides in England and Wales reached a *record high* in 2016 (MoJ, 2017). England and Wales has significantly in excess of 80,000 prisoners and the *highest imprisonment rate* in Western Europe (Prison Reform Trust, 2017).

Systematic recording of prison suicides began in 1978 (Walker and Towl, 2016: 19), although categorising and counting custodial deaths is a contentious issue (Liebling, 1992; Razack, 2015). Since then suicide rates have varied over time, but adult male prisoners have a rate between five and six times in excess of the general population, whilst female prisoners' rate is 12–20

[12] Defined here as internal and external oversight bodies. There is an array of such bodies, in the public sector and in civil society (see Seddon, 2010). Chapter Four provides a further explanation.

times higher than in the general population[13] (Fazel et al, 2017: 946; Towl and Crighton, 2017: 16). Prison Service Instruction 64/2011 covers, over 70 pages, the overall management of prison suicide and self-harm, using the Assessment, Care in Custody, Teamwork (ACCT) document. Prison Service Instruction 07/2015 (Early Days in Custody) is also particularly relevant.

All prisoner deaths in England and Wales are now formally investigated by, at minimum, the police, the Prisons and Probation Ombudsman (the Ombudsman/PPO) and the Coroner, as explained in Chapter Two. The Ombudsman has investigated the circumstances of all prisoner deaths since April 2004, to support the UK's compliance with Article 2: specifically the need for independent investigations into all custodial deaths. Her Majesty's Inspectorate of Prisons (the Inspectorate/HMIP) routinely follows up recommendations from Ombudsman investigations (PPO, 2017a: 8), thus contributing to the UK's international obligations under the Optional Protocol (HMIP, 2017: 1). Yet, despite the relatively developed investigatory framework and designated NPM in England and Wales, there has been surprisingly limited scholarly commentary about any aspect;[14] for example, 'although coroners fulfil an important function for state and society, they are notable for being underresearched by academics' (Baker, 2016: 170).

[13] See, for example, Dye (2011) and Walker and Towl (2016) regarding gendered suicide rates.

[14] Kendall (2018) considers volunteer Independent Custody Visitors that monitor police detention as part of the NPM. There is some grey literature. The charity INQUEST has published useful reviews: Goldson and Coles (2005) provide an introductory account of post-death investigations, published very shortly after the Ombudsman's remit being extended to deaths in custody and focused on limited numbers of *child* deaths in penal custody. Shaw and Coles (2007) illustrate *families*' experiences of death in custody investigations. Coles and Shaw (2012) propose an expanded framework for learning from death in custody inquests.

Generally, 'criminological scholarship is found … wanting on any wholesale attention to theorising death investigation' (Scott Bray, 2017: 147). Inquests into custody deaths received some attention in the 1980s and were critiqued for reproducing the assumption that 'people who choke on their own vomit, hang themselves in a distressed state or die unattended in a … cell are not controversial so long as they are checked every half-hour' (Scraton and Chadwick, 1986: 101). The deceased's individual pathologies deflected concern from systemic failures, negligence and brutality: 'friends and relatives of the deceased attend the inquest … they become disillusioned and embittered by a procedure which relies on … building … negative reputations of the deceased in often unsubtle attempts to justify acts of negligence or brutality' (Scraton and Chadwick, 1987: 95; see also Gilligan and Pratt, 2013; Razack, 2015; Gooch, 2016). It is important to consider whether these critiques still hold today, given the introduction of Article 2, which has 'more exacting' requirements than domestic case law and 'made more effective … remedies available to the bereaved relatives of persons who die in the custody of the State' (Owen and Macdonald, 2015: 122), as detailed in Chapter Two. Are prisons monitoring and investigation bodies just legitimising the operation of state power, by appearing to secure transparency and safeguarding detainees, whilst being ineffective and deflecting attention from systemic failings (Kendall, 2018)? Or have they any value for detainees and their families?

Although hundreds of prison suicides have been investigated since the investigatory framework was expanded in 2004, they have received little analysis. In prison suicide scholarship, Liebling (1998) provides an introductory account of prison staff experiences of suicide and coroners' inquests, but this significantly predates the 2004 expansion of investigations. Liebling (2007: 424) notes that 'the inquests (which are held before a jury) and investigations (which are conducted by the … ombudsman) are arduous, time consuming and expensive, and ... often leave behind considerable ill-feeling' but does not consider in detail how they operate or to what ends. Liebling and Ludlow (2016: 238) conclude their comments on suicide, distress and the quality of prison life by stating that Ombudsman investigations 'provide a starting point for much-needed analysis' into recent increases in prison suicide. This call has not yet been heeded. In their monograph *Preventing Self-injury and Suicide in Women's Prisons*, Walker and Towl (2016: 125–127) allocate just two sides to inquests and half a side to Ombudsman investigations (Walker and Towl, 2016: 135). In *Suicide in Prisons*, Towl and Crighton (2017: 110–112) allot three sides to the Ombudsman.

More broadly, Seneviratne (2010: 21) reviews the Ombudsman in general terms, concluding that 'the fatal incidents remit is not standard Ombudsman territory (of investigating complaints), but this is clearly important work'. Behan and Kirkham (2016) examine tripartite prison accountability structures in England and Wales, the Republic of Ireland and Scotland, including systems of monitoring, inspection and complaints adjudication, but do not consider post-death investigations. Seddon (2010) argues that general prison inspection is an under-researched tool for improvement and suggests a research agenda, which has at the time of writing received only three English-language citations in studies of police accountability.[15]

This book draws on data gathered through extensive document analysis and original interviews with stakeholders. These subjective case studies offer rich description of individual, situated lives and deaths rather than representative or generalisable analysis of every response following every prison suicide. Prisoners, prison staff, police, ombudsmen and coroners vary. These data were focused on suicides, so may have selected a particularly dire sample of cases within the prison estate. Crucially, these data were gathered during an extended period of rising prison suicides. Suicides in English and Welsh prisons

[15] See Google Scholar.

rose by 69% between April 2013 and 2014 (MoJ, 2014: 8). By the end of the 2016 calendar year, suicide rates had doubled since 2012 and a record high of 119 self-inflicted prisoner deaths was recorded, alongside a record level of 354 deaths in prison custody (MoJ, 2017: 2). My arguments might have been very different if my fieldwork had been undertaken during a less acute prisons crisis. For example, in those circumstances potential staff stigmatisation of prisoners, and organisational cultures and practices (Baker, 2016: 200) might have been more problematic, requiring different recommendations for oversight than presented here.

Document analysis of over 100 Ombudsman fatal incident investigations into prisoner self-inflicted deaths was undertaken.[16] Cases were gathered in reverse chronological order and the sample contained deaths from 2012 to 2017. Although there were significantly more than 100 suicides in these five years, reports appear with varying degrees of delay. For example, 12 June 2014 saw suicides at HMPs (Her Majesty's Prison) Bullingdon and Winchester, but the Ombudsman published the report on the Winchester death online just over one year later, on 17 June 2015.[17] The Bullingdon death was published online on 24 October 2017, over three years and four months later.[18] This creates some bias in the sample, as it means, for example, that the most complex and potentially blameworthy deaths that occurred close to the time of writing were not represented. However, less recent complex deaths did feature, such as the

16 The Ombudsman has a searchable online database of investigations. www.ppo.gov.uk/document/fii-report/.

17 www.ppo.gov.uk/document/fii-report/.

18 Although this does not relate to published final reports, the Ombudsman has gone from 86% of reports being late in 2011 to almost every fatal incident draft report being on time in 2016 (PPO, 2017: 14).

self-inflicted death of a 15-year-old in HMYOI (Her Majesty's Young Offender Institution) Cookham Wood in January 2012.[19]

The sample overwhelmingly contained adult male prisoners, although a small number of child and female deaths were represented. Different groups of prisoners can have specific risks and needs (see, for example, Ludlow et al, 2015: xiii regarding imprisoned women and Harris, 2015 regarding 18–24-year-old prisoners) but deaths amongst different groups are investigated in the same way. Coroners' Reports to Prevent Future Deaths (PFD) were also examined.[20] Publicly available Ombudsman and Coroner reports provide a helpful, albeit mediated and delayed account of individual deaths.

In depth, semi-structured interviews[21] were undertaken on a confidential basis with 16 diverse stakeholders during 2016–2017, including varying public and voluntary sector investigation and monitoring bodies and bereaved families. Quotations from bereaved families are marked throughout the text to indicate their positionality. This is a topic for which finding interview participants can be challenging,[22] however the interviews valuably supplement the document analysis of a large sample. In addition, I co-organised a prison suicide prevention roundtable at HMP Altcourse (England) in May 2016,[23] organised an international, interdisciplinary 'Death in Punishment' conference in October 2017 in Sheffield

[19] https://s3-eu-west-2.amazonaws.com/ppo-prod-storage-1g9rkhjhkjmgw/uploads/2014/12/G207-12-Death-of-a-boy-in-hospital-Cookham-Wood-25-01-2012-SID-14-17.pdf.

[20] www.judiciary.gov.uk/subject/state-custody-related-deaths/.

[21] Ethical approval was granted by the University of Sheffield School of Law.

[22] For example, Sweeney et al (2018) gained nine interviews with prison staff after inviting 247 to participate. Although a different participant group to my study, the low participation rate is illuminating.

[23] www.prc.crim.cam.ac.uk/news/suicide-prevention-conference.

(England)[24] and gave the keynote lecture at the September 2017 Samaritans Prison Listener/Irish Prison Service annual conference at Wheatfield Prison, Dublin (Republic of Ireland).

This text focuses on prison because of the recent record number of prison suicides (MoJ, 2017). However, there are clear parallels between this prison suicide research and broader deaths (for example, homicide, 'natural') in other forms of detention, such as police (Baker, 2016; Angiolini, 2017), immigration (for example, Procter et al, 2013) and psychiatric (for example, Powell et al, 2000). Furthermore, there is a high rate of death in the early period after release from prison, particularly from drug-related deaths (Binswanger et al, 2007). Yet criminal justice deaths outside custodial settings are severely neglected (Phillips et al, 2017). I hope others will use my study as a springboard for further analysis of investigations following deaths in different detention institutions and geographical jurisdictions, being mindful that 'the best tests for humanity and decency are conducted in its dark places: in prisons, psychiatric hospitals, and in institutions for failed asylum-seekers' (Shaw, 2005: 3).

Defining prison suicide: "They're just as dead, whatever the motivations"

I refer to 'prison suicide' in this book, indicating all self-inflicted prisoner deaths regardless of intention. This section explores problems with the terminology of 'suicide' which should be borne in mind throughout the book, although the important broader discussion around prison suicide, self-inflicted death and potentially lethal 'manipulative' behaviour should be continued in future.

The seminal Durkheimian definition of suicide is 'the termination of an individual's life, resulting directly from a

24 www.sheffield.ac.uk/law/research/clusters/ccr/conferences/death_in_punishment.

negative or positive act of the victim himself, which *he knows* will produce this fatal result' (Durkheim, 1952: 44, emphasis added). Although there are many definitions across academic disciplines, 'one of the central elements of all definitions of suicide is the concept of intention' (Tait et al, 2015: 240). Within almost all jurisdictions based upon English Common Law, only a coroner can make an official finding of suicide, and evidence of intention separates suicides from deaths classified as 'accidental' or given 'open' verdicts[25] (Tait et al, 2015; Henden, 2017). The term 'self-inflicted death' is perhaps more appropriate for prisoner deaths, as it encompasses intentional and accidental deaths from a prisoner's own actions. But intention in completed self-inflicted deaths is often unclear, and confused and mixed intentions can be seen in completed and attempted self-inflicted deaths and amongst those who self-harm (Walker and Towl, 2016: 31). Furthermore, many prison staff refer to unintended, accidental deaths resulting from the prisoner's own actions as 'suicide' (Ludlow et al, 2015: 15).

The literature is awash with prison staff references to 'manipulative' and 'attention-seeking' prisoner self-harm or attempted suicide (Ludlow et al, 2015: 23; see also, for example, Walker and Towl, 2016: 115; Towl and Crighton, 2017: 143; Sweeney et al, 2018). Certainly prisoners can seek to manipulate staff, but dismissing potentially lethal behaviour as manipulative can reduce opportunities to monitor prisoners and may result in deaths. My interviews revealed further tensions in establishing suicidal intentions. On the one hand, participants considered that prisoners often didn't intend to take their own lives, but were desperate for help; didn't understand the potentially lethal implications of their actions (this seemed particularly relevant for

[25] Scandinavian countries do not require proof of intention for a verdict of suicide and their rates both in and out of prison are significantly higher than most countries (Liebling, 1992: 27).

younger prisoners); or were inherently incapable of exercising intent in the coercive, potentially unfamiliar prison environment:

> Alice: 'We are quite careful to talk about self-inflicted deaths and people taking their own lives rather than suicide because for a lot of families, the circumstances in which the person died, it wasn't a deliberate act it was a cry for help.'
>
> Trevor: 'In some young offender institutions I've worked for [...] I don't think some of these young offenders would have any sense of the levels of lethality of some of the things they were doing, so most of them wouldn't think they could hang themselves with a bed end the size of this table. I know they could.'
>
> Brian: 'Prison is a false environment and it's very easy to base your self-esteem and your opinions about your future [...] on the [...] environment [...]. It is quite hard sometimes, especially with young prisoners, trying to communicate to them that death is that final act, that you do this and it's all over [...] you are not coming back and you quite often find young people [...] talking about their funerals and saying they want to see the effect that their death will have on [...] the people around them.'
>
> Joanne: 'Prisoners don't have free choice about anything in prison, they can't make a free choice.'[26]

Prison suicide is part of a continuum of self-destructive behaviour, including attempted suicide and self-harm (Liebling, 1992: 63; Towl and Crighton, 2017: 39–51). Broadly, 'the causes

[26] Nevertheless, prisoners are considered to have sufficient autonomy to, for example, commit further offences whilst imprisoned, marry, have a religious conversion or pursue educational opportunities (Lazarus, 2004).

expressed by prisoners describing their activities as suicidal are the same as those causes relating to less lethal types of self-harm'[27] (Liebling, 1992: 63). Rather than stumbling over the potentially unknowable intentions of prisoners, it is necessary to understand that *'manipulative' behaviour can be or become self-destructive* and should not be dismissed. Foregrounding potential death rather than querying intention could save lives and reduce harm:

> Trevor: 'This person's serious and this one's not. That's what they say on my training. […] Let's suppose the hypothesis is true, that person's doing it to get […] someone's attention, albeit they don't intend on taking their own life. Well, the sort of motivation doesn't matter […] They're still dead. They're just as dead, whatever the motivations.'

The significance of this discussion is hard to overstate, given that prisoner self-harm in England and Wales reached a record high of 42,837 incidents in the 12 months to September 2017 (MoJ, 2018: 1), and that prison staff are crucial in identifying, managing and preventing suicide risk (Liebling, 1992). Staff can be helpful and understanding in response to self-harm, expression of suicidal intention and suicide attempts, but hostile or judgemental attitudes and reactions to self-harm and distress can exacerbate those conditions (Marzano et al, 2012; see also Cole-King et al, 2013). Staff training and capacity to manage self-harm, expression of suicidal intention and suicide attempts is therefore critical. It bears repeating that 'prison authorities exercise direct and enormous power over those who are imprisoned. This power shapes the conditions under which prisoners are held. These conditions not only determine the

[27] Although on occasion self-harm can have different functions and involve distinctive behaviours and histories than attempted self-inflicted death (for example, Fulwiler et al, 1997; Walker and Towl, 2016: 31–32).

quality of prisoners' lives but may also literally be a matter of life or death' (van Zyl Smit, 2010: 504). Developing this potentially lethal assumption of manipulation, barriers to prison suicide prevention are now considered: that is, suicidogenic discourses, institutional apathy and prisoner stigmatisation by staff.

Prison suicides in context: vicious cycles, institutional apathy and stigma

> Advocacy is representing or speaking for another person. That ... involves caring about the interests of another person. Many care and are effective advocates. Many also care who have not found an effective means for advocating. Many others care, but the weight of institutional apathy and chronic frustration in their previous efforts as advocates have led them to set aside their caring and become pessimistic about what can be done. (Paul et al, 1977: xi)

The causes of prison suicide are complex, and depend on the cumulative and interactive effects of situational and psychosocial factors (for example, Walker and Towl, 2016: 49). Certainly, some proportion of prisoners have a sustained and settled desire to end their lives (Pridmore and Pridmore, 2017) and some prisoners may exhibit neither substantive risk factors nor any indications that they intend suicide. However, my interviews indicated that individual suicides can trigger vicious cycles of suicidogenic discourses and practices amongst prison staff. These vicious cycles are underappreciated. Jeremy explained how suicides can have a 'deadening effect' on prison staff, creating institutional apathy and preventable deaths:

> Jeremy: 'Prisons that have individually had a lot of self-inflicted deaths [...] that has a kind of deadening effect so it will just be [...] "we just have a lot of self-inflicted

> deaths here, it is one of the facts". You say "actually here's a prison that seems to have a very identical population, it's a Victorian ruin like yours but they don't, what's the explanation?" [...] When you get lots of deaths [...] people stop feeling as accountable, you know: "it's always like this, it is kind of what happens". [...] The fact that people feel with some justification that "it's not my fault" becomes "there is nothing I can do about it". So they may not be able to stop every death [...] but they could stop some of them [...] If you have someone who is clearly saying "I am feeling suicidal", is under regular observation and someone doesn't bother to do it properly then that was preventable, but it gets kind of lost, the ones that are preventable always get lost in all the ones that aren't.'[28]

Prison staff attitudes and cultures vary amongst individuals and their institutions (Parsloe, 1976; Liebling et al, 2010; Crewe et al, 2014). However, my data suggested that the high level of imported vulnerabilities amongst prisoners may lead prison staff to expect or accept some suicides, as Brian and Trevor explained:

> Brian: 'You record high numbers of suicides in prison but what you don't notice from the outside is the 350,000 or however many it is people who are going through [...] Prisons import a huge amount of suicide risk. [...] You are starting from the baseline of a very risky population [...] To get those vulnerabilities through jail in one piece and sending them out the door healthy...'

> Trevor: 'A prison officer who'd say they weren't too troubled, it was expected that they'd kill themselves

[28] This may also be the result of widespread, systematic indifference to 'othered' groups such as prisoners (Razack, 2015: 198).

> anyway, [...] that would not be seen as unusual in a canteen in a prison.'

It is possible that prison staff are extremely distressed by prisoner self-harm and suicide but do not admit this to colleagues due to perceived or actual stigma around accessing support (Walker et al, 2017; Sweeney et al, 2018). Regardless, the suicidogenic discourse and potential for institutional apathy (Paul et al, 1977) and staff burnout (Edelwich and Brodsky, 1980) that can follow suicides is problematic. The imported vulnerabilities amongst prisoners that Brian described could also mean that the threshold for triggering concern amongst prison staff is too high on occasion or diverges from policy. One investigator described their understandable 'deep frustration' about prisoners presenting at Reception with, for example, open neck wounds from self-harm but not being flagged as suicide risks. When examined with hindsight this is a clear cause for concern,[29] but this case is perhaps indicative of the generally high level of injury and risk amongst prisoners. It is possible that reception staff are accustomed to seeing prisoners who have, for instance, been in a fight and the majority are not suicidal:[30]

> Laura: 'Just the sum of the, like, *ugh*, *just* deep frustration that you feel when you read someone's huge numbers of risks and it's staggering the conclusions that people can draw. Like open neck wounds from self-harm the day before and "they seemed fine". It's just crazy [...] it is *so crucial* to have an informed assessment when someone

[29] See also Hancock and Liebling (2013) on organised knowledge and post-event constructions and inquiries.

[30] Further research could examine why prisoners are flagged as at risk of suicide, and whether those processes keep those individuals safe. See also Ludlow et al (2015: 40) regarding high levels of ACCT and potentially unrealistic Ombudsman expectations, such as that all prisoners with any history of self-harm should have an ACCT opened upon arrival.

> first arrives in prison [...] no kind of real weight is given to those really serious risk factors that they arrive with.'[31]

There is, therefore, a very fine line to tread between establishing lower thresholds for concern amongst prison staff dealing with chaotic conditions and multiple prisoner risks and needs daily, maintaining staff motivation in the event that death(s) occur(s); and balancing this against the fact that sometimes, even given the best prison conditions and care, prisoners will take their own lives. This fine line must be trodden in potentially challenging prison cultures, where prisoners are not necessarily considered worthy of help and care, are not necessarily believed, and may be violent towards staff responsible for their care and custody, as explored below.

The stigmatised, 'deeply discrediting' prisoner identity reduces the bearer 'from a whole and usual person to a tainted, discounted one' (Goffman 1963: 3). Crewe (2012) considers the male prisoner hierarchy and prisoner on prisoner stigmatisation of sex-offenders, 'grasses' and heroin users. Rowe (2011: 578) notes that, institutionally, prisons reflect a stigmatising 'spoiled identity' to prisoners and considers recurrent staff stereotyping of female prisoners as 'generically criminal'. Prisoner stigmatisation is, however, not a substantive feature of the suicide prevention literature.[32] Liebling (1992: 233) notes the 'language of contempt' used by prison staff and inmates alike towards prisoner distress - for example, 'manipulative', 'slashers', 'cutters' - but ascribes this to a functional attempt to 'avoid confronting the realities of pain and desperation'. Language of contempt may however also be a display of contempt and intended or perceived stigmatisation. In the specific context of Indigenous deaths in

31 See also McKinnon and Finch (2018) on health screening risk assessments in police custody suites.

32 See Chamberlen (2016) on female prisoners' self-harm scars as stigmatising symbols of deviance and imprisonment.

Canadian custody, Razack (2015: 30) notes that inquiries 'often acknowledge instances of neglect displayed by individuals but dance around the idea of racism and colonialism as its root cause. Dehumanization is never a part of legal explanations'.

The lack of attention to stigmatisation in suicide prevention is peculiar given that stigma is 'one of the key organising concepts at the heart of the sociology of punishment' (Lageson and Maruna, 2018: 113) and that 'the relationship between punishment and stigmatisation is rooted in some of the canonical texts of punishment and society, including the work of Durkheim, Mead, Becker, Kai Erikson, and Erving Goffman' (Lageson and Maruna, 2018: 114). Nevertheless, for suicide prevention 'relationships between staff and prisoners are key. Prisoners need to feel supported, cared for and able to confide in and trust staff. Prisoners described a culture[33] where, on the whole, distress was not believed or responded to with compassion' (Howard League, 2016b: 1). This disbelief may be partly explained by stigmatisation. My interviews indicated that staff stigmatisation of prisoners could be a *significant yet underreported* driver of prison suicide:

> Trevor: 'Prison officer culture is one of the biggest problems of suicide that's unreported. […] Treating prisoners with contempt. Telling them to go and kill themselves. If they say they feel like taking their own lives, say, "well why should I care?" […] Those are the things that happen in prisons. […] In public sector prisons in particular […] some prison officers will struggle if a member of the psychology team comes on to a wing and says "I'd like to see Mr so and so". They will say, "the only Misters here are us. They're not, they're names and numbers". This, to my mind, is showing contempt for people as individuals.

[33] As noted, prison staff attitudes and cultures vary amongst individuals and institutions.

> [...] That is incompatible with working with people who are feeling suicidal. So I think prison officer culture starts from a premise of basic contempt for prisoners. [...] That's not say there aren't good prison officers.'

> Debbie: 'There is [...] that underlying culture in prison which staff said was extremely difficult to change, which is the idea [...] that you are dealing with like the scum of the earth and they don't deserve better. [...] That was [...] contributing to risk because [...] people aren't believed and they are seen as manipulating, self-harm is constructed as an act of manipulation as opposed to distress.'

All prison staff, and also, I suggest, prison overseers and penal policy makers, are vulnerable to being captured by the approach of the 'wrong sort of prison officer'. Prisoners are all humans, but:

> Dave: 'The wrong sort of prison officer approaches their task saying, and I've been told this, "what you have got to remember is all these young lads, they are either murderers or rapists" and in a sense that is probably true, but that's ignoring the fact of why are they there, why did they get there, what led them to that because it's not usually their first offence, but also you still have human rights duty towards them because they are in your custody and care, but they are dismissing, well actually they do not matter because they are probably not very nice young men.'

Potential staff stigmatisation of prisoners needs to be considered with care. Certainly some staff do everything in their power to support despairing prisoners: 'some prisoners described how prison staff had provided fantastic support, looking out for them and regularly checking in' (Howard League, 2016b: 5). Furthermore, prison staff already have high levels of psychological distress (Walker and Towl, 2016: 130–134; Sweeney et al, 2018) and good staff morale is important for successful prisoner treatment (Liebling, 1992: 243). Nevertheless, staff stigmatisation of prisoners and its effects appears worthy of consideration and certainly may be important for suicide prevention efforts.[34] Whilst staff suspicion of prisoners is understandable to some extent, this suspicion may also lead staff to treat prisoners unfairly, dismiss potentially lethal behaviour as 'manipulative' and limit staff appreciation of prisoners' dynamic suicide risk factors. Previous work has illustrated that only about a quarter of prisoners who die by suicide were identified as at risk (Liebling, 2007: 426), and not believing prisoners may be one explanation for this low detection:

> Debbie: 'Quite a few [...] talked about [...] not being believed and this idea because you are in prison you must be a liar. [...] You must be a liar throughout your life because you have committed a crime. [...] One of them [...] was pregnant, she came into labour and no one would believe her, and she said [...] "if [...] I wanted to kill myself how will someone believe me because they are not even believing me when there was something physical?" [...] They said this that this was the kind of experience [...] you just weren't believed.'

Indeed, a fatal incident report into a death at HMP Winchester in January 2014 described a prisoner prescribed oxybutynin medication to prevent bedwetting (PPO, 2014a). The prisoner attributed the bedwetting to sleeping in a shared cell in prison,

34 Future scholarship could usefully consider whether staff stigmatisation of prisoners varies with race, ethnicity, gender and so on, and how this intersects with suicide prevention practice.

having 'been in care as a child and [...] seen a lot of violence'[35] (PPO, 2014a: 11). His medication prevented him providing a urine sample for a drug test on 16 October 2013, which healthcare and prison staff accepted as a valid reason. When the same situation arose a week later, the prisoner's inability to provide a urine sample saw him charged with a disciplinary offence, found guilty at the subsequent adjudication, losing his prison job and being downgraded from the highest level of incentives and earned privileges, meaning he lost gym time, a television, visits and all of his earnings for a prolonged period of time (PPO, 2014a: 5, 21). As the prisoner smoked, leaving him with no income for a prolonged period left him 'vulnerable to illicit behaviour in order to get by' (PPO, 2014a: 21). The Ombudsman found that the adjudication was fundamentally flawed because the prisoner was not able to question the reporting officer's evidence or offer any mitigation to the charge (PPO, 2014a: 5, 12). Whilst the prisoner was alive, he became very frustrated about not being able to comply with drug tests and worried about the implications for his parole hearing (PPO, 2014a: 6). On 6 December 2013, the prisoner told his substance misuse key worker that 'he should not have been found guilty' at the adjudication and 'felt "pigeon-holed" as a liar' (PPO, 2014a: 14). He hanged himself from his cell window on 3 January 2014 (PPO, 2014a: 6). The prisoner's father believed that 'the finding of guilt at the adjudication in October had been a major concern for his son as he had worried about how it would affect his sentence progression' (PPO, 2014a: 7). This was clearly an unjust adjudication, but it illustrates the potentially lethal implications of prisoners not being believed. More generally, if prisoners

[35] See also Howard League (2016b: 2): 'The impact of trauma in childhood, e.g. witnessing a murder, suicide or being the victim of sexual abuse was compounded by long periods spent alone in prison thinking. One prisoner discussed how being locked in their cell at night anticipating the morning wake-up call evoked memories of witnessing abuse in a children's home'.

are too rarely believed this can undermine the central tenet of a liveable life: being recognised in relationships with others as significant and worthy (Harbin, 2015: 160).

Relatedly, a report into a death at HMP Pentonville in December 2014 described a prisoner who, after having his television removed, became very distressed and repeatedly rang his cell bell. One interaction with an officer involved the prisoner saying 'I am going to fucking kill myself', to which the officer allegedly replied 'Do it. If I care' (PPO, 2015d: 14). The officer told the Ombudsman that if the prisoner 'had threatened to kill himself it would have been to get something done, rather than as a serious statement of intent' (PPO, 2015d: 14). The prisoner hanged himself from the window bars 'during the 24 minutes it took to answer his last cell bell' (PPO, 2015d: 21). Difficult acute situations can arise and cause staff to struggle to manage, thus creating delays, but the potentially lethal implications of not believing prisoners expressing suicidal ideation must not be dismissed.

Without refuting that many excellent members of prison staff care deeply about their prisoners and save lives every day, there is an important further discussion needed about how to care for stigmatised individuals in stigmatising institutions who may have done horrible things, indeed may appear to be "not very nice young men" (as interview participant Dave said) and may present challenging behaviour over sustained periods. How can we recognise the feelings of prison staff charged with caring for these individuals? How can we enable staff to recognise that these individuals are, regardless of their (alleged) crimes, humans who have needs? This discussion has relevance for the post-suicide investigations that are this book's focus, but could have far broader implications reaching into daily prison life.

In terms of challenging behaviour, the co-incidence of violence towards others and self-harm is recognised in prisoners.[36] Male prisoners who assault others in prison, damage property and set fires are more likely to self-harm (Slade, 2018). Almost 40% of female prisoners who self-harm are also violent (Kottler et al, 2018). Despite recognition of this co-incidence and its clear relevance to prison safety, 'quantification and clinical discussion are lacking' (Kottler et al, 2018: 2). Managing those who are harmful and vulnerable is challenging, as explained in an interview:

> Trevor: 'There's a level of task complexity, of understanding that if someone is aggressive, for example, and violent potentially, they're probably more at risk of suicide than someone who's not. […] You're violent, you know, so therefore I can't think of you as vulnerable because I'm feeling a bit threatened by you.'

Psychiatrists have noted the value of being able to be honest about, recognising and *working through negative feelings* - such as towards obese patients - with supervisors or colleagues (Yalom, 2017). Prison staff must experience negative feelings towards (some) prisoners. Every individual in the world has biases. Indeed, it is hard not to react negatively to those who are violent towards you and your colleagues. Whilst some prison cultures may facilitate discussion of these feelings, others may not enable recognition and resolution of negative and difficult emotions towards prisoners. Indeed, one fatal incident report described staff wilfully blinding themselves to prisoners' offences, which is a missed opportunity for suicide prevention. The fatal incident report into a death at HMP Liverpool in April 2014 criticised

36 Co-incidence of violence and self-harm is also recognised beyond prison populations. Repeated exposure to physically painful and/or fear-inducing experiences can create both the capability to engage in suicidal behaviour and the development of risks for violence (Slade, 2018). Being a perpetrator of violence may have a stronger link with later self-harm with strong suicidal intent than being a victim of violence (Jordan and Samuelson, 2015)

how 'few of the staff questioned him about the circumstances of his arrest and murder charge. It is worrying that some of the staff said that they preferred not to know the reasons why someone was in prison – although this is a crucial factor when assessing risk of suicide or self-harm' (PPO, 2015a: 17). The Ombudsman concluded that prison staff should have recognised this prisoner's risk when he arrived and begun suicide and self-harm prevention procedures based on his risk factors: being charged with an extremely violent offence against his partner, suffering from depression and other mental health problems, withdrawing from alcohol, being held on remand, being in the early days of custody and his daughter's suicide the year before (PPO, 2015a: 5, 17).

Prison suicide prevention work is clearly challenging. *Fundamentally, some proportion of prisoners are in an inappropriate environment to manage their mental health needs* (for example, Rutherford and Taylor, 2004; Forrester et al, 2013).[37] Prison staff are charged with detecting suicide risk factors amongst a generally risky and needy population, in what can be chaotic prison conditions: 'although forensic administrators are not technically mental health service providers, the residents of prisons and jails are clearly at elevated risk for suicide, and staff at these facilities should be properly trained in recognizing suicide risk' (Smith et al, 2008: 789). Staff must work to prevent suicide amidst the inevitability that sometimes prisoners will die by their

[37] 'The police often fulfill the role of gatekeeper in deciding whether a person with mental illness who has come to their attention should enter the mental health system or the criminal justice system. Criminalization may result if this role is not performed appropriately' (Lamb et al, 2002: 1266). 'In 2005 between 3000 and 3700 prisoners were estimated to present with acute mental health needs such that they required urgent transfer to hospital … These numbers significantly exceed the capacity of existing psychiatric services and they are one reason why in many areas there have been long delays in transferring mentally ill prisoners to hospital' (Forrester et al, 2013: 327).

own hand. Prison cultures may position prisoners as requiring suspicion and being unworthy of help and care, prisoners may have committed abhorrent crimes and vulnerable prisoners may attack and disrupt those expected to care for them. This important discussion has far-reaching implications for general prison and suicide management.

Given the particularly challenging nature of prison suicide prevention work, it is problematic that those working with prisoners appear not to be enabled at a basic level to keep them safe. Chapter Two will demonstrate that prison staff are set up to fail in suicide management: Prison Service Instructions and Orders protect the MoJ but do not enable staff to protect prisoners. Indeed, Prison Service Instruction 64/2011 (MoJ, 2013) 'lists no fewer than 26 risk factors for suicide (page 18) and a non-exhaustive list of eleven possible triggers (page 20). There can be few if any prisoners to whom none of these factors or triggers applies. Indeed, the mental health criterion would include over half the entire prison population' (Shaw, 2017: 11). The Ombudsman recently reported that 'investigations rarely identify a fundamental lack of care or compassion[38] among those who support the suicidal … Too frequently, I do find failures of management, weak procedures, poor information sharing, a lack of joined up working, gaps in training and poor emergency responses' (PPO, 2017a: 9). The inquest into Sean Plumstead's death in HMP Winchester on 15 September 2016 made a Report to Prevent Future Deaths, which noted that:

> targets for … the Introduction to Suicide and Self-Harm Prevention … training are failing to be met and if anything the ratio of prison staff with the appropriate skills is reducing rather than increasing. This means that the risk of prisoners at risk of self harm and suicide may not be

[38] But see Razack (2015), Baker (2016) and Kendall (2018: 22–23).

> recognised by staff who have had no such training with whom they come into contact.[39]

The target was to train only 80% of staff.[40] The Coroner also noted that Carillion staff were employed in prisoner-facing roles without any training in suicide and self-harm prevention. As such, when Mr Plumstead asked a Carillion worker in the prison's clothing exchange about the best way to kill himself, this was neither recorded nor reported.[41] Similarly, the inquest into Christopher Talbot's death in HMP Preston on 28 November 2014 made a PFD report, which noted:

> the Supervising Officer on duty at Reception when Mr Talbot arrived had never received training in her duties but merely gained experience by shadowing another officer. It did not appear that any written material was provided so as to inform her of her duties, including the Prison Service Instruction 'Early Days In Custody, Reception In, First Night In Custody And Induction To Custody' or a guidance document summarising the main provisions of the Instruction. Lack of such written material and reliance solely on shadowing as a means of training might bring about a position where bad habits are proliferated or important considerations missed.[42]

The next section considers the consequences of (potentially avoidable) prison suicides such as these.

[39] www.judiciary.gov.uk/wp-content/uploads/2017/12/Sean-Plumstead-2017-0316.-Amended_Redacted-1.pdf.

[40] See Walker and Towl (2016: 105-107) for further information on suicide prevention training for prison staff.

[41] www.theguardian.com/society/2017/oct/19/hmp-winchester-inmate-staff-suicide-sean-plumstead.

[42] www.judiciary.gov.uk/wp-content/uploads/2018/02/Christopher-Talbot-2017-0427.pdf.

The consequences

> The impact of a suicide in prison is profound for the family, for prisoners, for prison staff and for all those who knew the individual who died. The emotional costs include pain, grief and lost quality of life. (Howard League, 2016a: 1)

Prison suicides have substantive consequences for other prisoners, prison staff and prisoners' families, which this section introduces and Chapter Three further explores. There is surprisingly little research about effects of prison suicide on other prisoners,[43] although witnessing distress, self-harm and attempted suicide must affect other prisoners. Sean Plumstead's cellmate at HMP Winchester had only moved in that day and found him 'hanging by his neck from a ligature … attached to one of the bars of the cell window'.[44] It took 10.5 minutes for staff to respond to the emergency cell bell. Whilst the inquest recognised that this delay exceeding the required five-minute response could have contributed to Mr Plumstead's death,[45] it was also likely to have been a traumatic wait for the cellmate. Vilhelmas Borkertas hanged himself in HMP Pentonville on 21 November 2016. His cellmate woke to use the toilet, switched on the light, found Mr Borkertas hanging from the window

43 'The impact of a death of someone with whom they were living had a profound impact on some young adults' (Harris, 2015: 173). 'Prisoners reported feeling unsafe when locked in a cell with someone who was more vulnerable. It sometimes exacerbated their own feelings of vulnerability: … "... I can't talk to them ... they are in a worse state than me ... that doesn't help me ... I am with them all day and I have no one to talk to ..."' (Howard League, 2016b: 4).

44 www.judiciary.gov.uk/wp-content/uploads/2017/12/Sean-Plumstead-2017-0316.-Amended_Redacted-1.pdf.

45 www.theguardian.com/society/2017/oct/19/hmp-winchester-inmate-staff-suicide-sean-plumstead.

bars and rang his cell bell. The cell bell was answered *21 minutes* later.[46]

Prison staff can also be affected by suicide and attempted suicide (Liebling, 1992; Walker et al, 2017; Sweeney et al, 2018). The death at HMP Winchester in January 2014 involving medication to prevent bedwetting highlighted this. When the prisoner was found hanging, a night orderly 'did not go into the man's cell as he did not want to see his body' (PPO, 2014a: 16). This orderly 'had dealt with a number of self-inflicted deaths of prisoners at Winchester some 20 years earlier and he was still struggling to cope with the trauma of what he had seen. At the time, he had not received any workplace support' (PPO, 2014a: 16). The night orderly 'had been anxious about returning to work the evening after the 2014 death, but felt he could not say so for fear of seeming weak. Several staff said they had experienced flashbacks and other distressing symptoms in the aftermath of the man's death' (PPO, 2014a: 17). It appears that the situation had not improved in 20 years, as other officers involved in the 2014 death 'were negative about the support at the prison on the day … no manager had asked them if they were all right or discussed with them whether they felt able to work that evening' (PPO, 2014a: 17). One officer 'described the post-incident care as badly handled and wanted someone to recognise that what they had experienced was traumatic and not a petty incident' (PPO, 2014a: 17). The Ombudsman concluded that the night orderly 'appears to have been too damaged by trauma from earlier incidents to have operated fully effectively' (PPO, 2014a: 23). 'As the night orderly officer's unfortunate experience showed, the effects can be long-lasting if staff are not given timely and effective support after an incident. In turn, this can impact on the safety of prisoners in future emergencies' (PPO, 2014a: 24).

46 www.judiciary.gov.uk/wp-content/uploads/2018/02/Vilhelmas-Borkertas-2017-0342_Redacted.pdf.

Furthermore, the friends and family of those who have died in our prisons are not guilty of any crime, but are left to cope with the loss of their loved ones in controversial circumstances. After his inquest, Sean Plumstead's mother said:

> 'It was also hard to hear about the delay in the cell bell being answered. I know that I will forever wonder about what might have happened had staff got to Sean within the time they were supposed to. My hope now is that another family will not have to go through what we have, although the evidence we have heard at the inquest indicates that HMP Winchester does not learn lessons.' (Reported in *The Guardian*)[47]

Hennie Fenlon was 15 when her dad Robert died in 2016 and has publicly explained her loss. Robert was one of the 18 men who took their lives at HMP Woodhill between May 2013 and December 2016, as explored in Chapter Two. Hennie stated that prison governors should:

> 'Look after the prisoners better and if they're feeling down, let them talk to someone, put them on a suicide watch, watch them 24/7, because it's not them that has to deal with everything at the end of the day, it's me, I'm the only thing really he's left behind. I never thought that I would've been picking up my Dad's ashes.' (Reported on Channel 4 news)[48]

---

47 www.theguardian.com/society/2017/oct/19/hmp-winchester-inmate-staff-suicide-sean-plumstead.

48 www.youtube.com/watch?v=d_PObW-0nAQ.

Karen Revell's 18-year-old son Greg died on his second night in the now closed HMP Glen Parva[49] in 2014, an institution which the Inspectorate deemed unsafe.[50] She said:

> 'He had visible scars on his neck from the first time […] he did it with shoelaces […] they were very deep. […] You couldn't miss them […] I would have had him on suicide watch given his previous history.' (Reported on BBC Newsnight)[51]

Dean Saunders' parents, partner and young son have lost their loved one, and must come to terms with the widely condemned circumstances of his death at HMP Chelmsford on 4 January 2016.[52] Dean was arrested whilst in a mental health crisis and trying to harm himself, but was not diverted into healthcare by police or prison, despite the fact that 'all those involved in his care agreed that prison was not an appropriate place for him' (PPO, 2016a: i). His parents said:

> 'We were being "told he's fine, he's safe, he's secure" […] when a professional holds you by the hand, looks you in the face and says "we will do everything to keep him safe, he's in a safe place", you've got no option but to take that for face value and you think that they are going to do that. Obviously they fell short. […] On the Monday morning, they all come in and gone "right, we haven't got the staff, we haven't got the resources, we haven't got the money, it's costing too much, off constant watch".' (Reported on Channel 4 news)[53]

49 www.leicestermercury.co.uk/news/local-news/demolition-crews-set-move-after-421918.

50 www.psa.ac.uk/insight-plus/blog/why-prison-suicides-matter.

51 www.youtube.com/watch?v=vu2N_jrGn5o.

52 www.bbc.co.uk/news/uk-england-essex-36369948.

53 www.youtube.com/watch?v=9aTUkY-1a9s.

The Coroner's PFD report regarding Mr Saunders noted that the 'head of healthcare treated financial considerations as a significant reason to reduce the level of observations'.[54] Following the inquest jury's critical narrative verdict, the prison's healthcare provider Care UK quit its contract, stating that it 'had attempted to resolve issues at Chelmsford Prison but the level of resources the prison planned to make available were "insufficient"'.[55]

These human harms are explored further in Chapter Three. In addition, the hundreds of millions of pounds that prison suicides cost annually must be acknowledged (Howard League, 2016a). The economic costs of suicide are profound, although comparatively few studies have sought to quantify them.[56] All suicides are economically costly due to inquests and police investigations, although prison suicides are dearer because of the Ombudsman investigation, more complex inquests involving a senior coroner and legal representation for public agencies, additional prison staffing costs to attend investigations and cover potential staff sickness, and prison contributions to funeral expenses (Howard League, 2016a). One interview participant noted that a single death in custody could cost more than half a million pounds:

> Dave: 'We started doing some work. "Please don't go there", type reaction, of what is the cost of a death in custody and it's probably at least half a million pounds, maybe more and you know if you are looking at several hundred deaths that quickly mounts up as serious money. [...] So if you used that £500,000 to prevent the death.'

54 www.judiciary.gov.uk/wp-content/uploads/2017/03/Saunders-2017-0056.pdf.

55 www.bbc.co.uk/news/uk-england-essex-38689048.

56 www.pssru.ac.uk/blog/population-level-suicide-awareness-training-and-intervention/.

Having outlined the vicious cycles that can spiral from prison suicides, the next section considers how prison suicides have been more effectively prevented in the past and contextualises recent increases in suicide against reduced prison staffing to cut costs in the short term.

Safer Custody

From 2001 to 2004, the Prison Service developed an extensive Safer Custody programme incorporating initiatives including prisoner peer support, mental health in-reach services and full-time suicide prevention coordinators in local prisons given their relative riskiness (Liebling and Ludlow, 2016: 225–226; Walker and Towl, 2016: 37). Following this considerable investment of policy attention and resources, suicides dropped in 2005 for the first time in a decade (Liebling, 2007: 424) and significantly lowered rates of prison suicide were then seen until 2011 (Liebling and Ludlow, 2016: 226). Although the easiest way to reduce numbers of prison suicides is reducing the prison population, these improvements demonstrate that *it is possible to reduce prison suicide*. Yet the sustained increases seen from 2012 to 2016 (MoJ, 2018: 2) demonstrate that important gains can quickly be undone. Safer Custody's success was sadly followed by record-breaking numbers of prison suicides in 2016 (MoJ, 2017) and incidents of self-harm in 2017 (MoJ, 2018).

It is interesting that these increases were not checked by the introduction of additional safeguards: for example, the UK ratified the Optional Protocol to the Convention Against Torture in December 2003 and established its NPM in March 2009.[57] The three-tier Ministerial Council on Deaths in Custody was announced in July 2008 following the Fulton Review of the Forum for Preventing Deaths in Custody: establishing a Ministerial Board, Independent Advisory Panel and practitioner

57 https://apt.ch/en/opcat_pages/opcat-ratification-70/.

and stakeholder group (Towl and Crighton, 2017: 103). Further information about Article 2-compliant investigations is provided in Chapter Two. However, the latest prison policy document at the time of writing notes:

> Levels of self-harm and self-inflicted deaths are also rising. … These changes have come after a period of change for the prison workforce as a result of making efficiencies. … Frontline operational staff reduced from 29,660 on 31 March 2012 to 23,080 on 31 March 2016. As violence has increased it has become harder to retain existing staff, thus creating a vicious cycle of staff pressure and violence. While it was right to seek to operate prisons more efficiently [sic – it wasn't], the destabilising effect of changes in the operating environment, such as the introduction of new psychoactive substances … means we must now reconsider staffing levels. Our analysis shows a statistical correlation between the numbers of staff and the level of violent incidents. (MoJ, 2016: 41)

These staff cuts were, however, widely predicted to lead to increased violence, self-harm and suicide,[58] and my interviews demonstrated that Ministers were explicitly warned of this:

> Jeremy: 'It is about population increases and staff reduction. […] We don't have enough staff for the population we have. […] What happened was a result of political

[58] Note that staff shortages are also implicated in broader prison deaths. For example, John O'Meara died at HMP Wormwood Scrubs on 29 March 2016 from a catastrophic respiratory failure. He died in part because 'insufficient staffing levels in the Conibeere Unit led to inadequate medical supervision, specifically the omission of the medical monitoring and failure to complete full vital signs checks on the day of his death'. www.judiciary.gov.uk/wp-content/uploads/2018/03/John-OMeara-2018-0012_Redacted.pdf.

> decisions, it was absolutely the case that Ministers were warned explicitly by me and by other people, that if you do this it will lead to increased violence and self-harm and people made a political decision that that didn't kind of matter.'

> Dave: 'The process that was started in 2012, which was very hard line, I mean you know people kept saying "this is going to happen, this is going to happen".'

Prison staff numbers are not the only factor affecting suicide rates, but interview participant Laura explained that HMP Woodhill, which has the highest number of suicides in England and Wales since 2013, and is further examined in Chapter Two, had serious shortages of experienced staff:

> Laura: 'Safety of prisons is just totally compromised and there are less [sic] staff and […] the turnover is really high and the prison that I keep mentioning, Woodhill, […] is […] often cited as really struggling to keep a core of experienced staff and I think that's a microcosm of what is a broader problem.'

Whilst safeguards and mechanisms for investigating prison suicides have multiplied since 2003, suicide prevention appears to have been affected by both lack of prison staff and fewer experienced prison staff. Post-death investigations have severely limited influence over these important aspects of prison conditions, as explored throughout this book.

Book structure

This chapter has described the global importance of analysing post-prison suicide investigations and introduced the case study of England and Wales, which has a substantive prison monitoring and post-death investigations framework but recent record numbers of prison suicides. The case study of England and Wales is used to provide the first analysis of these investigations in this book. This chapter has detailed the importance of acknowledging that 'manipulative' prisoner behaviour can be lethal and recommended foregrounding potential death rather than querying prisoners' potentially unknowable intentions. It has outlined the underappreciated roles of suicidogenic discourses, institutional apathy and prisoner stigmatisation in suicide prevention, and explained the particular difficulties of suicide prevention work. It has provided a preliminary exploration of the effects of prison suicide on other prisoners, staff and bereaved families, and outlined that suicide prevention was significantly more effective from 2005 to 2011, which was predictably overturned by swingeing staff cuts.

The next chapter explores *how* post-suicide investigations operate in England and Wales, describing the police, Ombudsman and Coroner investigations that usually form the Article 2-compliant investigation and also considering potential criminal prosecutions and Health and Safety Executive (HSE) activity. It explores the suicide cluster at HMP Woodhill as a case study to illustrate these investigations, their value and their limitations. It argues that these investigations provide no shortage of vigorous critique, but identifies a limitation in that Article 2 does not require that lessons be learnt and does not direct accountability to those with the capacity to implement said lessons. It challenges the discourse of lesson learning, which is unhelpful in many cases of prison suicide as it manufactures mystery around what are often entirely manifests and previously identified issues, and obfuscates the role of deliberate political decisions in creating those issues.

Chapter Three considers how the full complement of post-suicide investigations *are experienced* by stakeholders including prison staff and bereaved families. It highlights the burden that these investigations can impose on bereaved families and prison staff, raises concerns about the degree of scrutiny to which prison staff can be subjected given their limited agency, notes the hazy links between the findings of post-suicide investigations and suicide preventions and restates the need for accountability of political decision makers. A publicly resourced independent support service for bereaved families is suggested.

Chapter Four explores *what these investigations achieve*. Using the three elements of oversight mechanisms to guide analysis (directors, detectors and effectors), it demonstrates that prisons have no shortage of directors and detectors, but very limited effectors, both in relation to prison suicide and in general. It is difficult to establish the merit of post-death investigations because their failures are highlighted but their successes are not. The chapter demonstrates the value of post-suicide investigations, referencing the investigations which followed the deaths of Dean Saunders and Sarah Reed. The legitimising effects of prisons oversight mean that overseers have a *responsibility* to speak truth to politicians, which (arguably) outweighs any constraints in their remits. Prison overseers in England and Wales are more than legitimising functions that shore up state activity, but they could achieve significantly more by targeting the government succinctly, repeatedly and robustly. It is also for the rest of us to take up the argument that the situations in which Dean Saunders and Sarah Reed died were not aberrations, but foreseeable outcomes of marooning very sick people in prison. It is to be expected that internal prison administration will fail. This book provides example after example.

2

Post-suicide investigations

> There is a great responsibility on the police or prison authorities to ensure that the citizen in its custody is not deprived of his right to life.
> (Anand J, in *Nilabati Behera* v *State of Orissa* (1993) 2 SCC 746 at 767[1])

Introduction

This chapter examines how the post-prison suicide investigations operate over considerable timescales and explores their legal basis. Prison suicides, along with all deaths in compulsory state detention that are unexplained or related to violence and self-harm will automatically engage Article 2 of the European Convention of Human Rights (Skelton and Williams, 2016). Article 2 protects the right to life and was enacted in the UK by the Human Rights Act 1998 which 'significantly illuminated and extended the … State's obligation to take active steps to prevent suicide and self-harm in custody, to protect prisoners from life-threatening assaults, and to investigate those deaths in custody which raise arguable violations of the right to life[2]'

1 Cited in *Regina* v *Secretary of State for the Home Department (Respondent) ex parte Amin (FC) (Appellant)* [2003] UKHL 51.

2 Article 3 is also relevant and prohibits torture and inhuman and degrading treatment. (See also Thoonen, 2017.)

(Owen and Macdonald, 2015: 120–121). Article 2 consists of three broad obligations:[3]

- The positive obligation: the systemic and operational duty to take appropriate steps to protect life. The state is required to take all reasonable care to protect the life of a person involuntarily in its custody.
- The negative obligation: the systemic and operational duty to prohibit intentional and unlawful taking of life by state agents.
- The free-standing procedural obligation: the duty to investigate potential violations of the positive and negative obligations.

The threshold at which breaches of the positive and negative obligations occur is high. The *Osman* test[4] considers the unpredictability of human conduct, operational choices which must be made in terms of priorities and resources, and the need to interpret Article 2 obligations in a way which does not impose an impossible or disproportionate burden on the authorities. But only a reasonable suspicion of breach is required to trigger the free-standing procedural obligation[5] for an Article 2-compliant investigation into a death (Skelton et al, 2016). The procedural obligation is the primary focus of this chapter.

The form and nature of an Article 2 investigation varies across jurisdictions but must meet multiple criteria. The investigating authorities must act of their own motion. The investigation must be initiated promptly and proceed with reasonable expedition; be independent; be open to public scrutiny; involve the next of

[3] For full details of relevant case law please see, for example, Owen and Macdonald (2015: 120–126) and Skelton et al (2016: 98–99).

[4] *Osman* v *United Kingdom* (2000) 29 EHRR 245, 5 BHRC 293, [2000] Inquest LR 101.

[5] *McCann* v *United Kingdom* (1996) 21 EHRR 97, para 161.

kin to the extent necessary to safeguard their legitimate interests; and be effective. Effective means that the investigation must:

- be conducted in a manner that does not undermine its ability to establish the relevant facts;
- comprise or obtain sufficient expertise;
- secure the relevant evidence, including witness evidence;
- identify those responsible for the death;
- reach conclusions in the central issues that are tenable and convincing and identify any shortcomings in the operation of the regulatory system.
- ensure accountability of state agents and bodies.[6]

Most frequently in England and Wales, a Coroner's inquest together with police and Ombudsman investigations form the Article 2 investigation (Shaw and Coles, 2007: 21). An inquest usually discharges the investigative obligation but 'other remedies may have to be pursued to secure the punishment of those criminally to blame and to secure non-pecuniary damages for the bereaved' (Owen and Macdonald, 2015: 127). Although rare, the state's procedural obligation may also be discharged through a public inquiry, as eventually followed Zahid Mubarek's murder in 2000 in Feltham Young Offender Institution (YOI) (Owen and Macdonald, 2015). Failures in the investigative procedures may breach Article 2 and lead to damages being awarded to prisoners' dependants (Foster, 2005; Skelton et al, 2016). The series of investigators is now considered, including the police, HSE, Ombudsman and Coroner. These investigations are illustrated using HMP Woodhill, which had a cluster of 18 suicides from 2013 to 2016, triggering a particularly broad range of investigations. This chapter explores how government

6 *Jordan* v *United Kingdom* (2001) 37 EHRR 52; *Edwards* v *United Kingdom* (2002) 35 EHRR 19.

policies (including benchmarking) set staff at HMP Woodhill up to fail in suicide prevention work.

Police

Prison Service Instruction 64/2011 requires that prisons promptly notify the police and the Coroner of a death (MoJ, 2013).[7] Police approach all prison deaths as potential homicides,[8] and conduct a criminal investigation (National Police Chiefs' Council (NPCC)/PPO, 2015: 1–2). The scene of death should be secured and not interfered with prior to police arrival (NPCC/PPO, 2015: 3). Police investigations are generally given primacy over Ombudsman investigations to avoid prejudicing criminal or legal proceedings[9] (NPCC/PPO, 2015: 2). The Ombudsman may investigate in parallel with police, subject to parameters such as not interviewing people involved in the criminal investigation (NPCC/PPO, 2015: 2).

There are potential corporate manslaughter charges and prison staff are subject to prosecution for manslaughter, murder and health and safety offences, for instance. Death in custody referrals are dealt with by senior prosecution lawyers in the Crown Prosecution Service's Special Crime and Counter Terrorism Division. CPS lawyers advise investigating bodies such as the

---

7 Prison Service Instructions are not legally binding in themselves, but 'the extent to which the guidance … is fulfilled in any particular case will be relevant to any negligence claim against the prison, assuming that a duty of care has been established' (Owen and Macdonald, 2015: 315).

8 If a prisoner dies in hospital with a recognised illness or medical history, the death is treated no differently than a death in a civilian hospital. Where a prisoner dies in a cell and their death is 'believed to be due to natural causes i.e. heart attack', the police involvement is minimal 'other than securing evidence pending a post mortem result' (NPCC/PPO, 2015: 1).

9 The relationships between the Ombudsman and other bodies are set out in non-binding memoranda of understanding.

police and HSE,[10] and may prosecute given sufficient evidence. The Corporate Manslaughter and Corporate Homicide Act 2007 created a specific homicide offence for corporations, government departments and public bodies that cause death. Section 2(7) provides that a duty of care is owed to anyone detained at a custodial institution. Thus, from September 2011, Her Majesty's Prison and Probation Service (HMPPS) and private prison operators became potentially liable for prison deaths[11] (Doyle and McGrath, 2016). This Act is symbolically and practically significant because the law has struggled to ascribe fault to companies. However, enforcements have been lower than predicted, targeting small companies, rather than the complex organisations the Act was intended to address, and apparently obvious cases where guilty pleas were likely (Field and Jones, 2014). The Act has not yet been invoked for a death in prison custody and it is likely to 'prove extraordinarily difficult to subject HMPPS to criminal liability ... because the legislation imposes a requirement that the actions of senior management must have played a substantial role in the breach of duty resulting in death' (Doyle and McGrath, 2016: 166). This 'senior management' requirement fails to acknowledge the practical exercise of prison suicide prevention procedures by non-managerial officer and operational support grades (Doyle and McGrath, 2016: 162–163). As such, excepting an unusual situation where a prison death was directly attributable to an instruction given by a Governor/Director/Chief Executive, Deputy Governor/Director or Head of Function, it would be very difficult for the CPS to establish liability for corporate manslaughter (Doyle and McGrath, 2016). Prisons thus retain an ability to deflect liability, along with any large organisation with complex management and operational structures, because

10 www.cps.gov.uk/your_cps/our_organisation/sc_and_ctd.html.

11 Companies cannot form subjective intent so cannot commit murder in English law (Doyle and McGrath 2016: 155).

operational decisions are frequently assigned to lower levels of management (Griffin and Moran, 2010: 371).

It is extremely rare for a prosecution to follow a death in custody[12] (Shaw and Coles, 2007: 12). Joseph Travers was the first prison officer to be charged with gross negligence manslaughter, following the self-inflicted death of Ryan Harvey at HMP Woodhill in May 2015. Mr Travers was found not guilty in January 2018.[13] Previously manslaughter charges have not followed even when inquests have delivered verdicts of unlawful killing, such as in the restraint-related prison deaths of Omasase Lumumba (died 1991) and Alton Manning (died 1995). During a strip-search at HMP Blakenhurst, Alton Manning was asked to squat naked for a genital and anal inspection, allegedly assaulted an officer and was restrained by six or seven officers. Mr Manning was then carried, naked on his bottom half and in a neck-hold, along a corridor and suffered asphyxia.[14]

Where there is suspicion of a criminal offence and the matter is referred to the CPS, the investigation can become 'very lengthy and this long wait for a decision can be particularly stressful to all concerned'.[15] For example, Alton Manning died on 8 December 1995, the Director of Public Prosecutions made a decision not to prosecute any officers in September 1996, the inquest jury returned a unanimous verdict of unlawful killing in March 1998, the Director of Public Prosecutions made another decision not to prosecute in February 1999 and reaffirmed this in April 1999. Mr Manning's sisters won a judicial review of the decision not to prosecute in May 2000, the CPS undertook its fifth review of the

---

12 'There has never been a successful prosecution' of a police officer for manslaughter in connection with a death in police custody (Angiolini, 2017: 10).

13 www.bbc.co.uk/news/uk-england-beds-bucks-herts-42878661.

14 http://news.bbc.co.uk/1/hi/uk/734404.stm https://www.theguardian.com/uk/2000/may/04/race.world1.

15 www.cps.gov.uk/publications/prosecution/death_custody.html.

evidence in January 2002 and again decided not to prosecute.[16] At this point, seven years after the death, the family conceded. Mr Manning's sisters were bereaved again in January 2005, when another brother died in psychiatric hospital.[17]

Daniel Rooney (aka John Hughes) hanged himself in HMP Bullingdon on 26 September 2006.[18] He was on remand, charged with burglary. Shortly after his death, the case was referred for CPS consideration, resulting in suspension of the Ombudsman investigation. The CPS decision not to prosecute any prison staff was made 27 November 2007, when the bereaved wife was notified by letter and the Ombudsman investigation recommenced. The draft Ombudsman report was issued in May 2008 and the inquest took place in 2008. Following comments from the family's solicitors, the Ombudsman produced a new report, including an additional recommendation in June 2011. The National Offender Management Service (NOMS - as HMPPS was previously known) received a Crown Censure from the HSE in February 2012.[19] because the shower rail from which Mr Rooney hanged himself should have been attached to the wall with weaker fixings given the 'safer cell' designation.[20] The HSE is now considered in detail.

16 http://news.bbc.co.uk/1/hi/england/1782850.stm.

17 www.theguardian.com/uk/2005/feb/09/ukcrime.prisonsandprobation.

18 https://s3-eu-west-2.amazonaws.com/ppo-prod-storage-1g9rkhjhkjmgw/uploads/2014/07/086-06-death-of-a-male-prisoner.pdf.

19 Based on non-compliance with section 3(1) of the Health & Safety at Work Act 1974, and Regulation 5(1) of the Management of Health & Safety at Work Regulations 1999. www.hse.gov.uk/prosecutions/documents/crowncensures.htm#Crown%20Censure%2027%20:%20HM%20Prison%20Service.

20 www.independent.co.uk/news/uk/crime/bullingdon-prison-chiefs-censured-over-cell-death-6917267.html.

Health and Safety Executive

The HSE is primarily responsible for workplace health, safety and welfare but the Health and Safety at Work Act 1974 section 48 subjects HMPPS to health and safety law.[21] Although the health and safety standards for prison workshops and farms should be the same as those in the commercial sector, prisoners are only deemed to be employees when they are on work experience outside prison. As Crown employers, government departments cannot be prosecuted under the Health and Safety at Work Act 1974, so the HSE can only issue Crown Enforcement Notices and Crown Censures (Forster, 2012).[22] Private prison contractors are not immune from criminal prosecution. Crown Censures enable the HSE to censure a Crown employer for a breach of the Act which, but for Crown Immunity, would have led to prosecution with a realistic prospect of conviction. HMPPS has received three Crown Censures since 1999, including in Mr Rooney's case above.[23]

The HSE has also issued Crown improvement and enforcement notices responding to the Prison Service's preparation of risk assessments, largely under the Control of Substances Hazardous to Health Regulations 2002, dealing with, for example, poor control of microbiological risks arising from contact with blood and body fluids, and also under the Management of Health and Safety at Work Regulations 1992, dealing with the training of managers.[24] The Reporting of Injuries, Diseases and Dangerous Occurrences Regulations 1995 apply to prisons as to any facility or organisation used or occupied by the public. Prisoner

21 www.hse.gov.uk/foi/internalops/ocs/300-399/334_2/#para79-80.

22 The CPS brought health and safety prosecutions in the police shootings of Jean Charles De Menezes and Anthony Grainger as there was insufficient evidence to support homicide charges (Angiolini, 2017: 10).

23 www.hse.gov.uk/prosecutions/documents/crowncensures.htm#Crown%20Censure%2027%20:%20HM%20Prison%20Service.

24 www.hse.gov.uk/foi/internalops/ocs/300-399/334_2/#para79-80.

accidents are reportable where the accident arose from or was connected with the work of the prison. Prisoner suicides and assaults on prisoners are not reportable as they are not accidents, but assaults on prison staff are reportable.[25]

Standing Order 6A (15) allows for HSE prison inspections by appointment (Livingstone et al, 2008: 232). Inspectors identifying risks can use the Health and Safety at Work Act 1974 section 3. Prisons owe duties under section 3 to non-employees including other persons working in prisons, visitors and prisoners. Section 3 can deal with risks to prisoners while they are carrying out work in prison and are at risk from the work activities of others, but generally not problems arising due to confinement, such as cell conditions, since cells are not places of work.[26] The HSE will not engage in discussions about prison staffing levels, although if an agreed staffing level is set on the basis of a risk assessment carried out by prison management in consultation with staff, the staffing level should not be reduced without reviewing the risk assessment.[27]

Ombudsman

Before April 2004, prison deaths were investigated by the Prison Service's own investigators. Investigations tended to be 'extremely poor, limited in scope and focused narrowly on claims about individual pathology' (Shaw and Coles, 2007: 55). Since 2004, the Ombudsman has undertaken independent fatal incident investigations into all prisoner deaths to support Article 2 compliance. The Ombudsman has improved the independence of investigations, extended their scope, added a clinical review of the deceased's clinical care and enabled the deceased's family to raise questions and issues (PPO/Coroners' Society of England

25 Ibid.
26 Ibid.
27 Ibid.

and Wales (CSEW), 2012). There have however been concerns about the quality and independence of clinical reviews and late delivery of clinical reviews delaying Ombudsman investigations (Leach, 2011: 11; Harris, 2015: 182).

The Ombudsman is operationally independent of, although sponsored by the MoJ.[28] The Prisons and Courts Bill 2017 proposed a statutory footing for the Ombudsman, but this Bill fell with the 2017 general election. Although the Ombudsman has no powers to compel anyone to cooperate with investigations, in practice this has not created barriers, as services including HMPPS have guaranteed unfettered access and employee cooperation with the Ombudsman through memoranda of understanding[29] (PPO/CSEW, 2012: 1–2). The Ombudsman's remit includes all relevant matters for which HMPPS is responsible, or would be responsible if not contracted elsewhere (PPO/CSEW, 2012: 2). Ombudsman investigations aim to:

- establish the circumstances and events surrounding the death;
- examine whether any change in operational methods, policy, practice or management arrangements would help prevent recurrence;
- examine relevant health issues and review clinical care (in conjunction with NHS England/Healthcare Inspectorate Wales), including referrals to secondary healthcare;
- provide explanations and insight for bereaved relatives;
- help fulfil the Article 2 investigative obligation by working with coroners to ensure as far as possible that the full facts are brought to light and any relevant failing is exposed, any

[28] https://s3-eu-west-2.amazonaws.com/ppo-prod-storage-1g9rkhjhkjmgw/uploads/2017/04/PPO-Terms-of-reference-2017.pdf.

[29] However, UK public bodies can be subject to political interference. See, for example, Nick Hardwick's second appointment process as Chief Inspector of Prisons, which was criticised by the House of Commons Justice Committee in 2015 (Carver, 2016: 138–139).

commendable action or practice is identified, and any lessons are made clear.[30]

The Ombudsman aims to open and confirm their investigations into apparent self-inflicted deaths in writing within five working days of the prison's notification of death (PPO/CSEW, 2012: 3). The Ombudsman should make contact with the family within 15 days of the notification, offering the opportunity to meet to discuss concerns (PPO/CSEW, 2012: 3). The police share information with the Ombudsman (as soon as possible without prejudicing criminal proceedings), including photographs/videos of the scene of death; statements taken by the police; CCTV evidence; the post mortem report; the deceased's police antecedents, history and custody record; and the history of family liaison to date (NPCC/PPO, 2015: 3). All Ombudsman investigations into prison deaths include:

- examination of records;
- a clinical review;
- feedback to the establishment on the findings of the investigation;
- a statement on the cause of death;
- the majority of investigations also include audio-recorded interviews with staff and prisoners within a few weeks of the death[31] (PPO/CSEW, 2012: 3–4).

30 https://s3-eu-west-2.amazonaws.com/ppo-prod-storage-1g9rkhjhkjmgw/uploads/2017/04/PPO-Terms-of-reference-2017.pdf.

31 The Ombudsman does not now always conduct visits and interviews in cases of 'natural' death. See, for example, https://s3-eu-west-2.amazonaws.com/ppo-prod-storage-1g9rkhjhkjmgw/uploads/2017/08/M325-17-Death-of-Mr-James-McCann-Lincoln-20-01-2017-Nat-61-70.pdf. In this case, the investigator only obtained copies of relevant extracts from Mr McCann's prison and medical records.

Interviews are not conducted under caution because the Ombudsman does not have Police and Criminal Evidence Act 1984 powers, but interviewees check and sign the transcript (PPO/CSEW, 2012: 4). The draft report should be published within 26 weeks for non-natural cause investigations, although the Ombudsman does not have full control of timescales (PPO/CSEW, 2012: 5). Ombudsman draft and final reports are provided to the head of the prison authority, the bereaved family, the Coroner and NHS England/Healthcare Inspectorate Wales. Recipients have a period to draw attention to any factual inaccuracies. The Ombudsman publishes the final report on the website, but contacts the Coroner if the report is to be published before the inquest. The Ombudsman may make recommendations to bodies or individuals such as the prison authority or the Secretary of State for Justice. These authorities accept or reject recommendations within four weeks, detailing steps to be taken and timeframes.[32] The Ombudsman only monitors compliance with action plans when pertinent to a subsequent investigation at the same establishment, but provides all fatal incident recommendations to the Inspectorate to follow up (PPO/CSEW, 2012: 5):

> Jeremy: The Inspectorate 'would get a read out from […] incidents the [Ombudsman] were investigating even if a report hadn't been published. [The Inspectorate] would specifically […] look at whether recommendations the PPO had made were being implemented so each inspection report will have a paragraph on that.'

> Laura: 'The Inspectorate do pick up where people haven't done it [followed Ombudsman recommendations]. […]. [The Ombudsman] have a relationship with [the

32 https://s3-eu-west-2.amazonaws.com/ppo-prod-storage-1g9rkhjhkjmgw/uploads/2017/04/PPO-Terms-of-reference-2017.pdf.

> Inspectorate] where they sort of tell [the Inspectorate] you know [the Ombudsman are] *really* concerned about this prison. So if [the Inspectorate] are not thinking about going there in the next year or two, can you pop them higher up the list.'

These processes are not particularly effective however, according to the Ombudsman:

> It is not lack of knowledge, but a lack of effective action that is at issue […] My recommendations and thematic lessons rarely say anything new […]. Nor are prisons […] hostile or unsympathetic to what I have to say. Almost all my recommendations were accepted last year and an action plan put in place. […] But, too frequently, my colleagues at Her Majesty's Inspectorate of Prisons – who, on their visits, routinely follow up on my […] recommendations – found […] a lack of action. Worse, my investigators were often called to new fatal incidents, only to find that previous lessons had not been learned – with tragic consequences. (PPO, 2017a: 7–8)

This failure to learn lessons is perhaps unsurprising given that the Ombudsman points out failings but does not address solutions or the practicality of implementation. To their credit, and against a backdrop of substantial increases in demand for their services, the Ombudsman produces 'learning lessons reports' on thematic issues including, for instance, transgender prisoners and dementia.[33] In 'Learning from PPO Investigations: Self-inflicted Deaths of Prisoners', the Ombudsman notes, for example, that

> increased risk of suicide and self-harm must be considered when a prisoner is a suspected victim of bullying. Reports

33 www.ppo.gov.uk/document/learning-lessons-reports/.

> or suspicions that a prisoner is being threatened, bullied, or is vulnerable due to debt need to be recorded, investigated, and robustly responded to. The potential impact on the victim's risk of suicide and self-harm must always be considered.[34]

Whilst it is beyond the Ombudsman's remit to find prison management solutions, it is also short-sighted to presume that stating the risks of bullying would somehow create the requisite robust response, particularly given the apparent prevalence of bullying in prisons (for example, South and Wood, 2006) and the severe prison staff cuts experienced from 2012 (see Chapter One). It may be useful for the Ombudsman or Inspectorate to routinely outline what such a robust response to prison bullying might look like in practice, or to provide suggestions such as 'best practice' case studies.

After critiquing the lack of action in response to his recommendations, the Ombudsman's annual report expresses 'hope that prisons and their hard-pressed staff can emerge from a uniquely challenging and dispiriting period and address the well-evidenced concerns of independent scrutiny bodies such as mine' (PPO, 2017a: 8). This strategy places responsibility at once everywhere and nowhere. Prison suicide is, undeniably, everyone's concern (HMIP, 1999), but *whose responsibility is it* and *who is able to reduce it*?

Perhaps clearer responsibility and accountability will be created by the Urgent Notification process which had just been introduced at the time of writing. The process enables the Chief Inspector of Prisons to directly alert the Secretary of State for Justice about urgent and significant concern regarding a prison's performance. Although an urgent notification leads to a

---

34 https://s3-eu-west-2.amazonaws.com/ppo-prod-storage-1g9rkhjhkjmgw/uploads/2015/03/self-inflicted-deaths-2013-14-Final-for-publication-5.pdf, p 28.

published response and plan of action from the Secretary of State within 28 days, and a nebulous 'longer term plan for sustained improvement', the process is based on persuading government to act.[35] This section has introduced the Ombudsman, whose investigation informs the Coroner's inquest, which is now considered.

Coroner

A Coroner must investigate all deaths in compulsory state detention[36] under the Coroners and Justice Act 2009 section 1(2)(c). Where deaths arise in prison the Coroner has lawful control of the body and is the only person who may authorise a post mortem (PPO/CSEW, 2012: 5). Coroners formally open the inquest and contact the bereaved family within days (PPO/CSEW, 2012: 5). An inquest is a fact-finding exercise ascertaining who the deceased was and how, when and where they came by their death (McArdle, 2016). For suspected unnatural deaths in compulsory state detention, a Coroner's inquest must be held with a jury.[37] Coroners have statutory powers through the Coroners and Justice Act 2009 to compel document production and witnesses to give evidence (Wheeler, 2016). Inquests cannot determine civil or criminal liability, but may illustrate failings of individuals or agencies (PPO/CSEW, 2012: 5). Although inquests are inquisitorial, some adversarial procedures are incorporated and questioning may be robust (PPO/CSEW, 2012: 5).

---

35 www.gov.uk/government/publications/urgent-notification.

36 Including police, prison and military custody; immigration and mental health detention.

37 Coroners and Justice Act 2009 section 7(2)(a). The investigative duty in serious injury was also accepted by the state in *D* v *Secretary of State for the Home Department* [2006] EWCA Civ 143. Prisoner D was a known suicide risk, hanged himself in his cell and survived, but suffered permanent brain damage.

For prison suicides where there has not been a criminal trial or public inquiry, a *Middleton*[38] inquest is required[39] because the state may be responsible for the death (Skelton et al, 2016). *Middleton* means that, rather than the standard conclusion of 'by what means', the conclusion addresses 'by what means and in what circumstances' the deceased came to die (McArdle, 2016). Standard short-form inquest verdicts include natural causes, suicide (potentially whilst the balance of the deceased's mind was disturbed), accident/misadventure, industrial disease, death from dependence on drugs/misuse of drugs, (un)lawful killing, neglect[40]/self-neglect, homicide or 'open' (undetermined cause) (Carroll et al, 2012). Following *Middleton*, coroners can give the jury the option of providing a narrative verdict, because 'an uninformative jury verdict will be unlikely to meet … the purposes of an article 2 investigation'.[41] Narrative verdicts provide the circumstances of the death without assigning a single short-form category, potentially providing fuller accounts detailing key issues and establishing disputed facts (Carroll et al, 2012; Coles and Shaw, 2012).

Ombudsman reports and supporting evidence are provided to the Coroner, and introduce the circumstances and potential causes of the death (Skelton and Williams, 2016). The relevance of the Ombudsman report to the inquest was recognised in *R (L)* v *Justice Secretary*,[42] although their findings and conclusions were judged expressions of opinion that infringe the Coroner's function in Northern Ireland.[43]

---

38 Colin Middleton hanged himself in HMP Bristol in 1999.

39 Coroners and Justice Act 2009 section 5(2).

40 Neglect verdicts are distinct from civil negligence or breaches of a duty of care, which must be decided in civil court (Calthorpe and Choong, 2004).

41 [2004] 2 AC 182 paras 18–19.

42 [2009] 1 AC 588, para 18.

43 *Siberry's Application* (2) [2008] NIQB 147.

Where the inquest illustrates a concern that circumstances creating a risk of other deaths will occur, or continue to exist in the future, the Coroner is *obliged* to send a PFD report to organisations or persons with the power to take preventative action[44] (Cross and McArdle, 2016). The threshold is relatively low and reports can be issued even if the Coroner's concern is peripheral to the death (Cross and McArdle, 2016). However, coroners do not uniformly exercise their power to make PFD reports (Coles and Shaw, 2012; Mendas, 2012). Recipients must respond in writing within 56 days.[45] PFD reports must be sent to the Chief Coroner, who publishes the majority online in categories (Cross and McArdle, 2016).[46] Prison suicide PFD reports are found amongst broader 'state custody related deaths',[47] which include, for example, reports relating to members of the public who died jumping off a bridge in the presence of police.[48] If additional or conflicting information is discovered at inquest or a relevant PFD report is made, the Ombudsman may amend the report and reissue a draft for feedback (PPO/CSEW, 2012: 7).

The Coroner's remit is simply to establish 'by what means and in what circumstances' the deceased came to die, and to issue a PFD report to those able to take preventative action (Cross and McArdle, 2016). Coroners' external scrutiny of events and power to issue PFD reports means they are potentially significant agents of harm prevention, but critics argue that their potential is unrealised (Coles and Shaw, 2012; Mendas, 2012). However,

44 Coroners and Justice Act 2009 schedule 5, paragraph 7 and regulations 28 and 29.

45 Since the Coroners Rules were amended in 2008 (Coles and Shaw, 2012).

46 The MoJ Coroners Unit published nine bulletins summarising rule 43 reports until June 2013. The Chief Coroner published a single summary report providing statistical data in December 2013.

47 www.judiciary.gov.uk/related-offices-and-bodies/office-chief-coroner/pfd-reports/.

48 www.judiciary.gov.uk/publications/beverley-devanney/.

Coroner services are local and staffing levels and resources for administrative and judicial work are often inadequate (PPO/CSEW 2012). Coroners are 'wholly dependent on Local Authorities for their resources', there is no National Coroner Service and the system is 'under great pressure of resources, is "ad hoc" and largely dependent on a "grace and favour" relationship with other agencies' (Angiolini, 2017: 12; see also Baker, 2016).

The coronial system has received significant critique. Although some coroners copy PFD reports to the Inspectorate, the Inspectorate has reported difficulties accessing reports and HMPPS responses, limiting capacity to inform prison inspection criteria (Mendas, 2012: 38). Coroners tend to focus on local solutions in specific institutions rather than outcomes; for instance, they may request more extensive training in a specific institution rather than seeking to understand whether training is effective (Mendas, 2012). PFD reports may not always target the correct respondents. For example, Levi Cronin hanged himself on 20 September 2014, being the fourth prisoner to die from self-inflicted injuries sustained at HMP Highpoint since April 2013.[49] The Ombudsman 'raised serious concerns about the provision of mental health care at Highpoint, which we have been critical about before. A less pressed service, able to provide the level of care expected in the community, might have led to a more thorough multidisciplinary consideration of his risk and, possibly, a different outcome'.3[50] Note that the Ombudsman report is dated June 2015 but was uploaded on 27 April 2017.

[49] www.bindmans.com/news/jury-finds-a-series-of-interconnected-system-inadequacies-and-failures-cont.

[50] https://s3-eu-west-2.amazonaws.com/ppo-prod-storage-1g9rkhjhkjmgw/uploads/2017/04/K120-14-Death-of-a-male-prisoner-Highpoint-20-09-2014-SID-22-30.pdf, p 3.

The inquest concluded on 2 November 2017.[51] A PFD report dated 6 October 2017 noted:[52]

- Insufficient recording of information such as phone calls indicating concerns.
- Insufficient communication - for example, lack of information sharing between departments about Levi's welfare.
- Inadequate staffing levels within the mental health department and amongst prison staff - for example, the offender supervisor failed to see Levi in a timely matter, and there was a failure to follow up a mental health referral in a timely manner.
- Inadequate support and supervision to the mental health department.

The Coroner identified as matters of concern:

- Sharing of information between healthcare and prison staff.
- Recording of 'static' or 'historical' risk information in a form that would make it more readily accessible at a later stage.
- Ensuring that there is adequate and appropriate recording on prison wings of potentially significant events or changes in a person's mood or behaviour that could, if taken together, assist staff in their very difficult task of making risk assessments in the complex and challenging environment of a busy prison.

The Coroner did not directly address the staffing issue as a matter of concern, although it would appear to be implicated in and

51 www.bindmans.com/news/jury-finds-a-series-of-interconnected-system-inadequacies-and-failures-cont.

52 www.judiciary.gov.uk/wp-content/uploads/2017/11/Levi-Cronin-2017-0287.pdf.

affect the potential to resolve the other matters of concern. Staffing issues had not been resolved by the inquest, because the 2016–2017 Independent Monitoring Board[53] report for HMP Highpoint notes 'understaffing is impacting significantly on the ability of the prison to perform to its potential and make the identified improvements required. The Board seeks assurance from the Minister that funding for increased staffing will take into account the particular dynamics and contextual factors of Highpoint'.[54] Furthermore, the PFD report was sent to:

1. The Governor, HMP Highpoint, cc HM Prison and Probation Service.
2. The Head of Healthcare, HMP Highpoint, cc NHS England.

It is notable that the Governor and Head of Healthcare were the named respondents. Although the national authorities are copied in, they are not expected to respond. The responses are unfortunately not available online in any case.

Responses to PFD reports typically focus upon meeting the statutory obligation of responding within the 56-day time cap and emphasise circulating information, training and amending procedures locally, rather than seeing institutions seek to understand why existing frameworks have failed (Mendas, 2012: 38). 'Responses frequently state the national policy regarding the issue without instigating any efforts to learn' or addressing potential systemic concerns (Mendas, 2012: 24). Reliance on refresher training and recirculation of guidelines overlooks the fact that the original training and

53 Independent Monitoring Boards comprise volunteer lay people from the prison's local community and form part of the UK's national preventative mechanism, required by Article 3 of the Optional Protocol to the United Nations Convention Against Torture (Steinerte and Murray, 2009; Stern, 2010).

54 https://s3-eu-west-2.amazonaws.com/imb-prod-storage-1ocod6bqky0vo/uploads/2017/07/Highpoint-2016-17.pdf, p 4.

circulations failed to produce the desired results (Mendas, 2012: 25). Coroners' recommendations are not legally enforceable, there is nobody responsible for judging whether responses to PFD reports are appropriate and effective and no consistent mechanism for assessing implementation, meaning that an accountability deficit stretches across the criminal justice system and its overseers (Coles and Shaw 2012: 18; Mendas 2012: 28, 29). These elements are all exacerbated by PFD reports being generally perceived as a punishment by recipients rather than an opportunity to learn, and a lack of clarity about who should be engaging stakeholders to create improvements across the criminal justice system (Mendas, 2012). Coles and Shaw (2012: 8) note that there is 'no collation, analysis or central publication of narrative verdicts', meaning 'at most the local institutions or police force will learn the wider lessons from a narrative verdict, not … institutions of detention nationally'. This is also true for PFD reports. Nevertheless, even well-collated narrative verdicts and PFD reports are made some time after deaths, and this time lag can exceed four years (Mendas, 2012: 21).

This chapter has outlined the 2004 expansion of the Ombudsman to investigate prison deaths, the post-*Middleton* potential for a narrative inquest verdict, in addition to an extensive programme of prison inspections by the Inspectorate, prison monitoring by local Independent Monitoring Boards and the 2008 establishment of the Independent Advisory Panel and Ministerial Council on Deaths in Custody. Despite - or potentially enabled by (Razack, 2015; Kendall, 2018) - this substantive investigation and monitoring machinery, prison suicides rose dramatically from 2012, to 2016's record high.

Amidst national increases, individual institutions have had suicide clusters. These may occur randomly (Hope, 2009) or due to local conditions: prisons with higher proportions of remand and first-night prisoners are 'significantly more likely to experience suicide and self-harm than gaols with a stable long-term population' (Shaw, 2017: 32). The next section considers the case study of HMP Woodhill, which had 18 self-inflicted deaths between May 2013 and December 2016, and has triggered a range of investigations and responses, including a criminal prosecution, Ombudsman investigations and recommendations, Coroner inquests and PFD reports, a task force established in 2016 by the Deputy Director of Custody for the High Security Estate following an inspection, a judicial review, a civil claim and an independent review. Although HMP Woodhill is not the only individual prison where clusters have occurred, the number of deaths and variety of investigations and activities provide a particularly useful case study.

HMP Woodhill

HMP Woodhill is a men's prison near Milton Keynes in the South of England. It is a 'core local' prison, so remand and short-sentence prisoners form the majority of its population, but it also has a small number of category A (high-security) prisoners and a Close Supervision Centre for managing some of the most high-risk prisoners nationally.[55] Between 2011 and 2017, Woodhill has had 20 suicides, with deaths concentrated between 2013 and 2016, as illustrated by Figure 1.

55 www.justiceinspectorates.gov.uk/hmiprisons/wp-content/uploads/sites/4/2016/03/Woodhill-web2015.pdf.

Figure 1 HMP Woodhill suicides

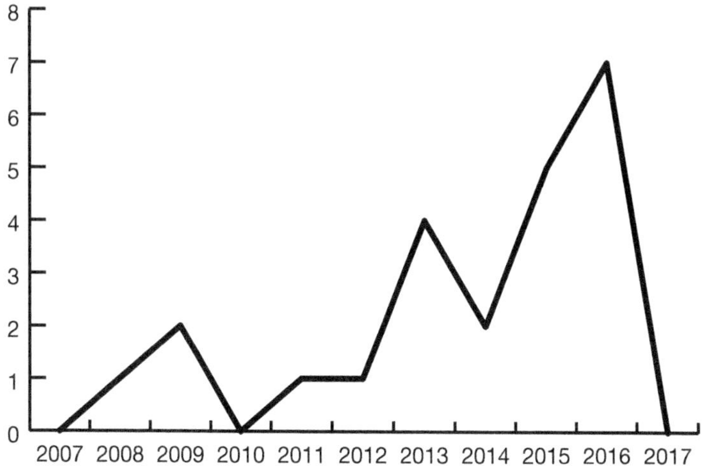

Note: See also Shaw (2017)

Table 1 summarises the 18 suicides since 2013. All prisoners were White British, apart from Michael Cameron ('Mixed White/ Black'), Ireneusz Polubinski ('White Other') and David Hunter ('Black Caribbean') (Shaw, 2017: 40).

As stated above, Joseph Travers was the first prison officer to be charged with manslaughter after a prisoner death.[56] Mr Travers was tried at the Old Bailey in January 2018 as it was alleged that he failed to remove a noose from Ryan Harvey, who hanged himself on 3 May 2015. Mr Travers argued that he did not know Mr Harvey had a noose and the jury took only 46 minutes to acquit, although they gave the judge a statement recording their 'view that the case has thrown up a number of appalling systemic failures to provide frontline staff with sufficient information as to the inmate's background'.[57] The usual Ombudsman and Coroner investigations also followed

[56] www.bbc.co.uk/news/uk-england-beds-bucks-herts-39107673.
[57] www.bbc.co.uk/news/uk-england-beds-bucks-herts-42878661.

each death. Table 2 summarises publicly available information about these investigations, as of 4 April 2018.

Table 1 Who died in Woodhill?

	Name	Death	Age	Status	Days in custody
1	Kevin Scarlett	22/05/13	30	Remand[a]	128
2	David Hunter	26/05/13	28	Sentenced	2
3	Sean Brock	10/11/13	21	Remand	3
4	Stephen Farrar	12/12/13	25	Remand	69
5	Dwane Harper	04/04/14	32	Sentenced	231
6	Jonathan White	14/10/14	37	Remand	244
7	Daniel Byrne	27/02/15	28	Remand	7
8	Ryan Harvey	08/05/15	23	Convicted[b]	14
9	Ian Brown	19/07/15	44	Convicted	180
10	Joanne[c]/Edward Latham	27/11/15	38	Sentenced	15 years, 11 months
11	Simon Turvey	29/12/15	27	Convicted	180
12	Ireneusz Polubinski	31/01/16	58	Convicted	26
13	Robert Fenlon	05/03/16	35	Remand	142
14	Michael Cameron	28/04/16	45	Remand	9
15	Thomas Morris	26/06/16	31	Sentenced	157
16	Daniel Dunkley	02/08/16	35	Sentenced	12
17	David Reynor	25/08/16	41	Remand	3
18	Jason Basalat	11/12/16	52	Remand	2

Notes: [a] Not convicted of a crime. [b] Unsentenced. [c] Ms Latham was born male but asked to live as a woman four months before her death. The Ombudsman referred to her as Joanne: www.ppo.gov.uk/app/uploads/2016/09/L215-15-Death-of-Ms-Joanne-Latham-Woodhill-27-11-2016-SID-31-40.pdf. The inquest was held under 'Eddie Latham, otherwise known as Joanne Marie Latham'. Ms Latham had also previously been known as Edward Adam Brown: www.theguardian.com/society/2015/dec/01/second-trans-prisoner-joanne-latham-apparently-takes-own-life-in-male-jail, www.bbc.co.uk/news/uk-england-beds-bucks-herts-35037388.
Source: Adapted from Shaw (2017: 40).

Table 2 Post-suicide investigations

	Name	Death	PPO report MM/YY[a] (online)	Inquest Ended[b]	PFD report made (online)
1	Kevin Scarlett	22/05/13	02/14 (18/03/15)	28/02/14	15/04/14 (15/04/14)
2	David Hunter	26/05/13	03/14 (06/03/15)		
3	Sean Brock	10/11/13	06/14 (01/09/14)	06/06/14	08/08/14 (08/08/14)
4	Stephen Farrar	12/12/13	06/14 (15/04/16)	01/08/14	29/08/14 (29/08/14)
5	Dwane Harper	04/04/14	10/14 (03/11/15)	02/15[c]	
6	Jonathan White	14/10/14	08/15 (22/06/16)		
7	Daniel Byrne	27/02/15	11/15 (21/01/16)		Yes[d]
8	Ryan Harvey	08/05/15	Criminal prosecution		
9	Ian Brown	19/07/15	04/16 (06/12/16)	26/04/16	26/05/16 (26/05/16)
10	Joanne/Edward Latham	27/11/15	08/16 (20/09/16)	09/16[e]	
11	Simon Turvey	29/12/15	09/16 (24/01/17)	24/11/16	13/12/16 (12/03/17)
12	Ireneusz Polubinski	31/01/16	09/16 (27/02/17)		
13	Robert Fenlon	05/03/16			
14	Michael Cameron	28/04/16	02/17 (19/05/17)	12/05/17[f]	
15	Thomas Morris	26/06/16	06/17 (29/09/17)	05/07/17[g]	
16	Daniel Dunkley	02/08/16	04/17 (03/05/17)	28/04/17	02/05/17 (15/08/17)
17	David Reynor	25/08/16			
18	Jason Basalat	11/12/16	12/17 (15/02/18)	17/11/17	27/11/17 (27/02/18)

Notes: [a] www.ppo.gov.uk/document/fii-report/. [b] www.judiciary.gov.uk/subject/state-custody-related-deaths/. [c] www.miltonkeynes.co.uk/news/prison-of-deaths-government-urged-to-intervene-at-woodhill-prison-1-6615773. [d] The PFD report was not online, but is referred to in paragraph 25 of *Scarfe & Ors, R (on the application of) v HMP Woodhill & Anor* [2017] EWHC 1194. [e] www.thesun.co.uk/news/1769797/transgender-female-prisoner-hanged-herself-at-all-male-prison-after-being-told-of-delay-in-receiving-make-up-brushes/. [f] www.itv.com/news/anglia/update/2017-05-12/suicide-verdict-in-inquest-into-death-of-inmate-after-prison-fails-to-protect-him/. [g] www.inquest.org.uk/tom-morris-inquest-conclusions

The Ombudsman has reported on 15 of the 18 Woodhill suicides in this cluster. Some deaths are subject to 'continuing police investigation' (Shaw, 2017: 6). These reports may exist in draft form but are not available on the Ombudsman's repository at the time of writing (April 2018). The Ombudsman has also published seven reports into deaths from natural causes and recreational drug use at HMP Woodhill since 2013. Many available Ombudsman reports on the suicides make worrying reading:

- 'While the man was identified as at risk of suicide and self-harm the day after he arrived at the prison, I am very concerned that his risk was not identified when he first arrived. [...] There was no systematic consideration of the man's risk factors, poor communication and poor handling of information, which led to staff underestimating his level of risk. I have raised most of these matters with Woodhill before' (re Daniel Byrne, PPO, 2015d: iii).
- 'I am concerned that there had been little effective implementation of previous recommendations about identifying risk and little evidence of staff engagement with Mr Turvey in the six months he was at Woodhill' (re Simon Turvey, PPO, 2016b: iii).
- 'Yet again, I raise concerns about the assessment and management of prisoners' risk of suicide and self-harm at the prison. The Deputy Director of Custody for the High Security Estate has, rightly, set up a task force to review and improve safety at the prison, clearly urgent action is required' (re Ireneusz Polubinski, PPO, 2016c: 1).
- 'Yet again, I raise concerns about the assessment and management of prisoners' risk of suicide and self-harm at the prison. The Deputy Director of Custody for the High Security Estate has, rightly, set up a task force to review and improve safety at the prison; clearly urgent action is required.

I await the update on the work of the task force which I have previously requested' (re Thomas Morris, PPO, 2017c: iii).

- 'Once again, our investigation identified significant deficiencies in Woodhill's operation of suicide and self-harm prevention procedures. We draw these deficiencies to the attention of the Deputy Director for Custody for the High Security Estate in light of his assurances on progress to improve safety at Woodhill' (re Daniel Dunkley, 2017b: iii).

The Inspectorate followed up Ombudsman recommendations from the earlier deaths in their unannounced inspection of Woodhill in September 2015. As one of four main recommendations, the Inspectorate suggested to the governor that:

> a prison-wide strategy and action plan to reduce the number of self-inflicted deaths and incidents of self-harm should be developed urgently … based on detailed data and trend analysis and include implementation of … Ombudsman recommendations. It should also include improvements in the quality of assessment, care in custody and teamwork (ACCT) case management documentation, and the lessons learned from internal investigations into life-threatening incidents.'[58]

The appropriateness of this recommendation will be considered later in this chapter. The prison's Action Plan, submitted on 9 June 2016,[59] noted that:

58 www.justiceinspectorates.gov.uk/hmiprisons/wp-content/uploads/sites/4/2016/03/Woodhill-web2015.pdf, p 63.

59 www.justiceinspectorates.gov.uk/hmiprisons/wp-content/uploads/sites/4/2016/03/HMP-Woodhill-Action-Plan.pdf.

> the Safer Custody Task Force was commissioned by the Deputy Director of Custody for the High Security Estate, building on good practice and lessons learned from other establishments' experiences. It will look to independently review existing procedures which relate to all aspects of safer custody including suicide prevention, self-harm management and violence reduction and make recommendations to remedy any identified weaknesses.

HM Coroner for Milton Keynes has opened inquests into all Woodhill suicides and PFD reports are available online for seven. Local news reported that Daniel Byrne hanged himself at Woodhill during Dwane Harper's inquest.[60] Although inquests are almost always held in open court, where the public may attend, it is surprisingly difficult to obtain information remotely about inquests where there was no media interest.[61] Whilst narrative verdicts are read aloud in open court, 'they are not collated as public records within any governmental agency' (Baker, 2016: 62). As such, the gaps in Table 2 do not necessarily indicate that an inquest has not taken place, or that a PFD report has not been made, but that this information is not available remotely.

Tom Osborne, Senior Coroner for Milton Keynes made a series of PFD reports relating to HMP Woodhill. Regarding Kevin Scarlett, Mr Osborne wrote to NOMS' Chief Executive stating: 'the prison service and healthcare did not assess the risk of Mr. Scarlett taking his own life, and I was informed that the

60 www.miltonkeynes.co.uk/news/prison-of-deaths-government-urged-to-intervene-at-woodhill-prison-1-6615773.

61 https://assets.publishing.service.gov.uk/government/uploads/system/uploads/attachment_data/file/363879/guide-to-coroner-service.pdf.

staff did not have access to a risk assessment tool or protocol'.[62] Whilst there are clearly defined and well-established tools for predicting violence and antisocial behaviours, for example, screening tools for suicide risk are not standardised or abundant (Gould et al, 2017). NOMS, however, replied that 'there is a comprehensive and effective set of systems for identifying that a prisoner is at risk, and that where this occurs a further detailed assessment is undertaken to ensure that all relevant factors are considered and risks identified'.[63]

Regarding Sean Brock, Mr Osborne wrote to the then Prisons Minister stating that 'a Governor from the prison during his evidence informed me that the number of prison officers at HMP Woodhill had recently been reduced by one-third. The reduction in numbers will in his view compromise prisoner safety and may put prisoner lives at risk'.[64] NOMS replied: 'the current identified total staffing forecast includes an agreed complement of Officers that are necessary to provide decent and secure conditions'.[65]

Regarding Stephen Farrar, Mr Osborne wrote to the then Prisons Minister stating that 'almost any risk assessment tool would have identified him as at risk. I was told there is no formal risk assessment tool in any of our prisons'.[66] NOMS replied: 'you raised similar concerns following an inquest … into a death at HMP Woodhill in May 2013 … Further action has also been

62 www.judiciary.gov.uk/wp-content/uploads/2014/07/Scarlett-2014-0174.pdf.

63 www.judiciary.gov.uk/wp-content/uploads/2014/04/2014-0174-Response-by-NOMS.pdf.

64 www.judiciary.gov.uk/wp-content/uploads/2014/11/Brock-2014-0381.pdf.

65 www.judiciary.gov.uk/wp-content/uploads/2014/08/2014-0381-Response-by-NOMS.pdf.

66 www.judiciary.gov.uk/wp-content/uploads/2014/11/Farrar-2014-0386.pdf.

taken locally at HMP Woodhill to address the matters about which you have raised concerns'.[67]

Regarding the death of Stephen Farrar, Mr Osborne wrote again to the then Prisons Minister and governor of Woodhill stating: 'I have concerns that … previous recommendations have been ignored … despite my previous PFD reports the number of suicides at HMP Woodhill continues to rise'.[68] NOMS replied:

> the Governor of HMP Woodhill, and the Deputy Director of Custody for High Security Prisons, have put in place processes and governance that will achieve successful action in response to the recommendations from [the Inspectorate] and the [Ombudsman], and the matters of concern raised in your … reports … This will bring the necessary improvements in safety.[69]

After this letter was sent on 22 July 2016, there were three more suicides. I agree with Shaw's critique that 'responses were treated as official correspondence rather than receiving a reply from the person to whom the reports were addressed. … A sense of ownership by Ministers and their senior advisers is better demonstrated if they are signed off at that level' (Shaw, 2017: 17). Moreover, the NOMS replies provided unfounded reassurances and deflections, rather than engaging with Coroner Osborne's comments.

Amidst this cluster of suicides, which were persisting despite the investigations, in November 2016 the families of Ian Brown and Daniel Dunkley were granted a judicial review. This challenged the governor of Woodhill and the Secretary of State

67 www.judiciary.gov.uk/wp-content/uploads/2014/08/2014-0386-Response-by-NOMS.pdf.

68 www.judiciary.gov.uk/wp-content/uploads/2016/09/Brown-2016-0200.pdf.

69 www.judiciary.gov.uk/wp-content/uploads/2016/05/2016-0200-Response-by-NOMS.pdf.

for Justice over failures to comply with their public law, common law and Article 2 duties to protect prisoners from suicide.[70] In February 2017, when the judicial review had been granted but not yet heard, the MoJ commissioned the independent Shaw review of the prevention of self-inflicted deaths and self-harm at HMP Woodhill. Although 'the commissioning note makes no mention of the Judicial Review brought on behalf of relatives of two Woodhill prisoners … it is not in doubt that the JR was the precipitating factor' (Shaw, 2017: 6).

The judicial review was heard at the High Court on 7 April 2017 and my information comes from the judgment.[71] When the judicial review was heard there had been 11 inquests, 13 Ombudsman reports and 18 suicides. The judicial review detailed similar failings in successive cases, citing the PFD report made in response to Daniel Byrne's death, for example: 'my concern is that reports and recommendations of the Ombudsman and indeed my own Preventing Future Death Reports have not been implemented by Woodhill prison and there needs to be an urgent review as to why the necessary measures to prevent suicides from recently admitted prisoners have not been implemented'. The critical legal issue was whether the suicides resulted from failure in the operation of the system (for example, failure by a prison officer or administrator), or failure of the system itself. The judgment noted that the number of errors did not matter, but their character did. The evidence demonstrated individual failings of understanding and compliance: not that the same mistake was made time and time again, which might imply that an issue had been identified, but that the system had failed to act.[72] National policies setting out prisons' obligations to prevent

70 www.theguardian.com/society/2016/nov/24/relatives-of-woodhill-prisoners-who-died-begin-legal-challenge.

71 *Scarfe & Ors, R (on the application of)* v *HMP Woodhill & Anor* [2017] EWHC 1194.

72 Ian Brown's family also sought a civil claim for damages relating to his death, which was transferred to the Queen's Bench Division following

self-inflicted deaths were considered to provide an appropriate system to protect life across the prison estate. Whittall (2017: 3) argues that the Court expressed a 'disturbing lack of judicial concern or criticism' about the manifest deficiencies in implementation of those Instructions: for example, the prison did not comply with the mandatory requirement of Instruction 64/2011 that all staff in contact with prisoners must be trained to at least ACCT Foundation level. The judgment also noted that even if system failures had been found, this is not a problem with which the Courts are equipped to deal in generality, *the solution to suicides in prison lying with those who have the unenviable task of managing prisons*. But who exactly are they? The difficulties at Woodhill were correlated with penal policies that were largely beyond the prison's control.

The Shaw review was delivered in the same month as the judicial review judgment. It stated that:

> the central concern of everyone to whom I have spoken has been the lack of consistent staffing ... The Benchmarking and Fair and Sustainable initiatives – that had seen senior staff leave and staffing levels fall – had demoralised the remaining staff. Some members of staff were now 'run ragged' and mainstream activities like ensuring canteen, Pinphones and property were routinely not sorted out ... Regularly at night there were insufficient staff to unlock a prisoner in distress. (Shaw, 2017: 11–14)

It concluded: 'the combination of reductions in the complement and difficulties of recruitment and retention have resulted in a completely unacceptable situation at Woodhill. These staffing pressures have been allowed to persist for far too long' (Shaw, 2017: 38).

the judicial review.

Once again, this raises the question of who is responsible for prison suicide and who is able to reduce it. Woodhill's staff, prisoners and their relatives have clearly suffered during this cluster. Regarding staff, the threat of Coroner's court and potential prosecution loomed large: 'everyone is frightened of being the next one in court' (Shaw, 2017: 14), 'the involvement of the police and CPS has had a significant impact upon the mood … of Woodhill staff. The unfavourable media reputation of the prison has also put pressure on staff' (Shaw, 2017: 6). The Ombudsman and Inspectorate have exerted significant pressure on the prison, as detailed above. Yet, as my interview participant Joanna explained about prison officers and suicide prevention in general:

> Joanne: 'It isn't their fault. They get what is it 10, 12 weeks training? And they are dealing with very complex people. They don't have the skills. And they have too many prisoners. […] Actually, they're not responsible for the fact that that young person, whoever it was ended up in custody, who maybe shouldn't have been there because they could have been in a secure placement or shouldn't have been in custody in the first place. I wouldn't want to see prison officers being attacked. But I think NOMS have responsibility, someone's in the care of the state, I mean the buck's gotta stop somewhere, they have responsibility to keep people safe.'

Furthermore, staff at Woodhill were *set up to fail.* It is true across the country that 'ACCT was designed at a time when the number of staff in prisons was significantly higher … and … the prison population was significantly lower' (Shaw, 2017: 36). The mandatory multidisciplinary first case review as directed by the Prison Service Instruction 'is simply a practical impossibility in Woodhill. I imagine this will apply to the vast majority of prisons. To put it at its mildest, it is not healthy for what is practicable to diverge so wildly from what is described as a mandatory action in a policy document' (Shaw, 2017: 36).

Woodhill's Independent Monitoring Board reported in 2017, for a third annual period, that the prison has functioned with restricted regimes[73] for the entire period, the serious staff shortages dating back to 2014 have 'only worsened' and the 'number of inexperienced staff is regularly between 40 and 60% per unit' (IMB, 2017: 4). This inevitably leads to prisoner boredom and isolation and 'the impoverished regime and reduction in staff time to engage with prisoners are major contributing factors in the increase in incidents of self harm and increase in violence' (IMB, 2017: 4). It bears repeating that prisoner 'vulnerability can be … alleviated in simple ways. Education, activity contact and concern might avert many crises' (Liebling 1992: 242). As my interview participant argued:

> Dave: 'The fundamental issue is if you don't have staff to do it, you can't do it. So if you have got, you know lots of Instructions, lots of good stuff […] about relating to individual prisoners and […] all things you are supposed to do if various warning flags come up but if you have got two prison officers supervising 100 people on a wing, they can't conceivably do that. […] Some prison officers, they will say that, "you know there is more we should have been doing" […] or "I remember when we used to".'

Woodhill has particular staff recruitment and retention difficulties due to 'the cost of housing, and the number of alternative jobs both in Milton Keynes itself and (30 minutes away by the fastest trains) in London' (Shaw, 2017: 8). It is also

[73] When the daily prison timetable is amended to reflect staff numbers. This can range from everything apart from meals and medication being cancelled to activities such as exercise, association, library and gym visits being cancelled.

notable that Woodhill has been multifunctional since the 1990s and during the recent cluster it was designated simultaneously 'as a core local, resettlement and high security prison', making it 'extremely challenging to manage' (IMB, 2017: 4). In late 2016 it was announced that Woodhill would transition to a category B training prison (Shaw, 2017: 8), but there are no indications that this has been completed. HMP Woodhill did not have any self-inflicted deaths in the 2017 calendar year. It is clear that post-suicide investigations appear to work slowly at best, and it is particularly concerning that suicides at HMP Woodhill only reduced *after already bereaved families sought a judicial review*.

Discussion

Commentators have noted an institutional unwillingness to approach deaths in custody as potential homicides or manslaughter, which allegedly affects the whole process from the police investigation onwards (Shaw and Coles, 2007: 12). This has purportedly created a 'culture of impunity and sends a clear message to police and prison officers that when deaths occur … they will not be called to account' (Shaw and Coles, 2007: 12). Such a culture of impunity would be enabled by the prisoner stigmatisation described in Chapter One. My research found limited evidence of prison staff impunity, but this may have been disguised by the extent of the staffing crisis. Anyone making a foray into prison suicide will be shocked by the stories that are too easily found, and something is clearly very wrong. Regarding the senior management requirement for corporate manslaughter prosecutions, various inquests, thematic reviews and PFD reports indicate that 'a substantial number of avoidable deaths in custody can be attributed to failures by lower-ranking staff to properly implement the correct policies and procedures where a prisoner has been identified at risk' (Doyle and McGrath, 2016: 163). But this does not necessarily mean that lower-ranking staff should be punished for these failures, unless they are malicious, and indeed in the implementation of ACCT *prison staff are set up to fail.*

HMPPS/NOMS reduced its budget by almost 25% between 2011 and 2017, with the cost of a prison place reducing by 20% between 2010 and 2016 (Prison Reform Trust, 2017: 5). Across England and Wales there are fewer staff looking after more prisoners, with 6,428 fewer staff looking after over 300 more prisoners since 2010, and the proportion of experienced staff declining (Prison Reform Trust, 2017: 5). A shortage of support staff means that officers often have to cover tasks such as answering phones, which diverts them from their work with prisoners (Prison Reform Trust, 2017: 5). Even given better conditions, prison staff arguably are inadequately trained to manage the needs of their population (Wacquant, 2009), which in England and Wales has overrepresentations of, for example, psychosis (Prison Reform Trust, 2017: 13).

Brutal treatment of prisoners is inexcusable. I certainly do not wish to apologise for institutional violence or racism, and it is important to remember that staff can go home at the end of a hard day, whereas prisoners cannot. But the conditions that prison staff must cope with are largely beyond their making. We need avenues for criminal prosecution of individuals and organisations, but we also need to consider the health of prisoners and prison staff (Walker and Towl, 2016). This Woodhill case study, and the next chapter, indicate that prison staff have been robustly held to account for their implementation of ACCT procedures, for example, which are impossible for them to fully implement given current conditions in many prisons. Successive policy makers are responsible for this. Chris Grayling's justice policies, including benchmarking, have played a significant role. Grayling's policies were criticised in March 2015 by the Justice Select Committee: 'the fall in staffing levels stemming from redundancies and increased turnover, which at their most acute have resulted in severely restricted regimes, are bound to have reduced the consistency of relationships between officers and prisoners, and in turn affected safety'.[74] The Committee also noted that the MoJ was publicly downplaying the significance of the 'sudden rise in self-inflicted deaths [...] and the potential role that changes in prisons policy might be playing in it'.[75] Woodhill's prisoners, staff and bereaved families have suffered during this cluster, and staff have been robustly held to account, but the cluster is clearly correlated with Chris Grayling's justice policies. I have come across no evidence of Mr Grayling or his successors being held to account in a manner similar to how investigations undertaken by the Ombudsman and coroners hold staff to account.

More generally, there is some scope to argue that the investigations following prison suicides are not Article 2 compliant. Many have argued for increased independence of investigators, such as the need to place the Ombudsman on a statutory footing to signal and safeguard its independence (for example, van Zyl Smit, 2010: 533; Harris, 2015: 182). The independence of coroners as local authority employees has been critiqued (Luce, 2007). Furthermore, prisons consistently fail to provide information about external support to bereaved families in the short-term aftermath of the death (Harris, 2015: 170; see also HMIP, 1999). In addition to being unfair, enduring difficulties around family participation and lack of automatic legal support for families could compromise investigatory independence (Smith, 2010). Bereaved families must undergo means testing to obtain funding for legal representation when the state has unlimited legal support, and families have to cover their own travel, accommodation and subsistence costs when attending inquests (Shaw and Coles, 2007: 53-54, 89-97). Angiolini (2017: 13) notes: 'for the state to fulfil its legal obligations of allowing effective participation of families in the

74 https://publications.parliament.uk/pa/cm201415/cmselect/cmjust/309/30903.htm.

75 Ibid.

process that is … not "empty and rhetorical" there should be access for the immediate family to free, non-means tested legal advice, assistance and representation immediately following the death and throughout the Inquest hearing'. But, without denying the importance of independence amongst monitoring bodies, and the relevance of any of the criticisms above, I would not expect such reforms to change the landscape of prison suicides. As this chapter demonstrates, the investigations following prison suicides in England and Wales identify lessons to be learned and offer no shortage of vigorous critique.

What none of the investigations do, perhaps unsurprisingly given that this is *not their remit* nor is it *required by article 2*, is identify *how these lessons could or should be learnt*, and designate an *official who is responsible for and has the capacity to* implement them. I suggest this official is the Secretary of State for Justice, as even autonomous governors have limited control over, for example, prison numbers, staff levels and secure mental health beds. I agree that there is a lack of clarity about who is engaging a range of stakeholders to create improvements across criminal justice and there is still no framework for the overview and scrutiny of findings and compliance with inquest verdicts and PFD reports (Mendas, 2012). However, I disagree that this means 'the current system is failing' (Coles and Shaw, 2012: 21). The current system is proven to be ineffectual at lesson learning and some proportion of prison suicides could be avoided, but it is not technically failing because no part of it is directly charged with this task. The House of Lords in *Amin* identifies the purpose of investigation under Article 2 as being:

> to ensure so far as possible that the full facts are brought to light, that culpable and discreditable conduct is exposed and brought to public notice, that suspicion of deliberate wrongdoing if unjustified is allayed, that dangerous practices and procedures are rectified, and that those who have lost their relative may at least have the satisfaction of

> knowing that lessons learned from his death may save the lives of others. (Quoted in Richards, 2007: 3)

These requirements are principally backwards facing, examining the circumstances leading to the death. Whilst rectifying 'dangerous practices and procedures' could have a preventative function, suicides can occur in the absence of positively dangerous practices and procedures. In my analysis, current investigations achieve these objectives. Lesson learning is clearly not particularly effective, but Article 2 does not currently require that it should be.

The Harris Review recommended that 'the powers of the PPO should be strengthened and arrangements to follow up actions following a PPO report and inquest findings should be enhanced' (Harris, 2015: 13). The charity INQUEST has long campaigned for 'a framework for the overview and scrutiny of findings and compliance' with Ombudsman and Coroner recommendations (Coles and Shaw, 2012: 21). Angiolini (2017: 13) recommends:

> establishing a national 'Office for Article 2 Compliance'. It would be accountable to Parliament, and tasked with the collation and dissemination of learning, the implementation and monitoring of that learning, and monitoring the consistency of its application at a national level. It should report publicly on the accumulated learning, and compliance arising from Inquest outcomes and recommendations. It should provide a route for bereaved families and community groups to voice their concerns.

Such an office makes sense and there are examples of good practice from elsewhere: such as in Ontario, Canada, where 'a specialist designated department monitors the implementation of the recommendations made by coroners' (Coles and Shaw

2012: 20). In Australia, government agencies have funded an online, publicly accessible database to assist with investigations and prevention strategies[76] (Coles and Shaw 2012: 23). These proposals, whilst obviously made with good intentions, irk me somewhat because they manufacture mystery around too often entirely manifest problems. Coroner Osborne said, at the conclusion of Daniel Dunkley's inquest in April 2017, when the Woodhill cluster seemed to have ended:

> We have not had a self-inflicted death at the prison since December 2016. Long may that continue. My hope is that we may go a whole year without a suicide. If that is achieved it will be in no small part due to lessons learned from Danny's death. I am hoping under the leadership of Governor Marfleet things will change but it is essential she is supported by the prison service and by the next government; otherwise Daniel will have died in vain.[77]

Coroner Osborne appears to have worked very hard to respond to the situation at HMP Woodhill and should be commended for his proactive efforts. However, discourse about learning lessons is unhelpful in many cases of prison suicide (such discourse is endemic and stated in *Amin*, not of Coroner Osborne's creation). Coroner Osborne's own PFD report noted that:

> prior to Mr Dunkley's death three referrals were made for him to undergo a full mental health assessment. None of the assessments took place prior to his death … Such assessments are vital to keep those suffering from

76 www.ncis.org.au.

77 https://www.milton-keynes.gov.uk/assets/attach/50957/Coroners%20Annual%20Report%202017%20-%20Final.pdf

> psychiatric problems … safe and an urgent review of the whole process is necessary.[78]

It is preposterous to posit that a single prisoner needed to die for the governor of HMP Woodhill, HMPPS, the Prisons Minister and the Secretary of State for Justice to learn this. Woodhill's Independent Monitoring Board's annual report covering 1 June 2014 to 31 May 2015 noted 'recruitment is a major issue. During the reporting year there were six and a half Band 5 vacancies, three Band 3 and one Band 6 for Mental Health' (IMB, 2015: 13). The Independent Monitoring Board's annual report covering 1 June 2015 to 31 May 2016 noted that 'recruitment remains a major issue. During the reporting year there were 10 Band 5 Primary Care vacancies, 3 Band 4 and 2 Band 5 Mental Health vacancies.' (IMB, 2016: 12). The Care Quality Commission report on Woodhill's healthcare found the primary healthcare team operated with a 51% vacancy rate in September 2016, and the mental health team was insufficient to meet the needs of Woodhill's population (Shaw, 2017: 10). Clinical psychiatrist Dr Elizabeth van Horn also resigned from her post at HMP Woodhill in April 2017, stating that staff shortages made improvements impossible and could lead to prisoners being locked up for 23 hours a day, which is in itself a major cause of mental health problems.[79] Mr Dunkley did not need to die in order for staffing issues and subsequent failed referrals at Woodhill to be identified and it is misleading to suggest otherwise: it is manufacturing mystery where there is none. It is also obfuscates the role of deliberate political decisions in creating the situation at Woodhill. Chapter Four expands on the issue of prisoner mental health illnesses.

---

78 www.judiciary.gov.uk/wp-content/uploads/2017/08/Daniel-Dunkley-2017-0147.pdf.

79 www.bbc.co.uk/news/uk-39967635.

Similar issues were also raised more broadly. The Equalities and Human Rights Commission (EHRC) undertook an inquiry into non-natural deaths in detention of adults with mental health conditions significantly before Mr Dunkley died. The EHRC emphasised (2015a: 6), in relation to increasing non-natural prison deaths since 2012, that the Inspectorate has cited worries about increased numbers of people being imprisoned and that both the Inspectorate and Ombudsman have voiced concerns about 'staff reductions, tougher regimes and less resources [sic] and possible links between the deaths and these factors'. The EHRC (2015: 6) recommended that 'those responsible for keeping prisoners safe should work together to understand and address these issues', again placing responsibility simultaneously everywhere and nowhere. As such, without disagreeing with critiques around investigatory independence, the most pressing concern is that there are too few staff to manage too many prisoners. This is the government's responsibility. Multiple oversight bodies have recognised and publicly recorded this point, but lessons can only be learnt if somebody with the capacity to implement them is listening (or is made to listen).

This chapter has illustrated the series of post-suicide investigators, including the police, HSE, Ombudsman and Coroner. It has examined the suicide cluster at HMP Woodhill to illustrate these investigations, their value and their limitations. It has concluded that the investigations are largely Article 2 compliant and there is no shortage of vigorous critique from investigators, but has also explained that Article 2 does not require that lessons be learnt and does not direct accountability to those with the capacity to implement said lessons. I have argued that this is a greater limitation in England and Wales than the more commonly recognised issues with family participation and independence. I have also argued that the discourse of lesson learning is unhelpful in many cases of prison suicide, manufacturing mystery where there is none. It is not a mystery when prisoners die with untreated mental health problems because the prison's mental health team is severely understaffed and has been for years. This problem is entirely manifest and was identified multiple times by multiple prison overseers. The discourse of lesson learning also obfuscates the role of deliberate political decisions in creating the situation at Woodhill (and beyond), where those staff remaining after swingeing benchmarking reforms were set up to fail. Overstretched staff could not follow prison suicide prevention processes as set out in the 70-page Prison Service Instruction 64/2011 (which technically expired on 31 January 2016), which makes reference to 17 further associated Orders and Instructions. Building on this chapter's consideration of prison staff stress caused by the looming Coroner's court and threat of prosecution (Shaw, 2017: 14), the next chapter examines how post-suicide investigations are experienced by prison staff and bereaved families.

3

Experiencing investigations

Introduction

Liebling (1998: 73) noted that critiques of prison suicide inquests tend to target the 'structural level' and fail to address 'the experiential level, where both staff and families' are located. However, 'both the structural and experiential levels should be fully addressed' (Liebling, 1998: 73). Since Liebling's comments, the investigations following prison suicides have evolved to include an additional Ombudsman investigation and clinical review. This chapter considers prison staff and prisoners' families' experiences of the full complement of post-prison suicide investigations. It highlights the burden that these investigations can impose on bereaved families and prison staff, raises concerns about the degree of scrutiny imposed upon prison staff given their limited agency, notes the unclear relationship between post-suicide investigations and suicide prevention and restates the need for accountability of political decision makers. A publicly resourced independent support service for bereaved families is suggested.

Staff and families may appear disparate and certainly should not be conflated, but there can be commonalities between their experiences through stages of bereavement (Lancaster, 2001). Both groups may be involved in routine investigations by the police, Ombudsman and Coroner, although families have more choice over whether to participate.[1] Investigations may be further extended in rare cases due to CPS or HSE involvement. Staff and families may give evidence to all of these bodies, or have multiple reports shared with them over significant time periods after the death.

The sequence of investigations that follow prison suicides can be a complicated and extended ordeal for families and staff. Experiences of these investigations bear recognition. There is, primarily, the effect of the death itself. Harris (2015: 162) notes the 'heart-breaking experiences of the families and friends of those who have died' and emphasises the importance of 'recognising the impact of a death on other prisoners and staff members'. Staff seem to be more commonly affected than unaffected by prison suicides, and prisoner suicide and self-harm are amongst the strongest contributors to the relatively high psychological distress amongst prison staff (Walker and Towl, 2016; Walker et al, 2017; Sweeney et al, 2018). Staff and family experiences of the investigations are triggered by and intertwined with the death, but the investigations create additional experiences, at what may already be a very difficult time. Other prisoners can also be affected by prison suicides (see Chapter One) and may also participate in investigations, for example by sending a letter to the Ombudsman.

Families and staff are not homogeneous entities. Prisoners may be estranged from (parts of) their families. Families can include parents, siblings, partners and children (perhaps with more than one partner). These individuals may be estranged from each other or have different points of view and experiences. Prison staff can be experienced, resilient individuals with good coping strategies and confidence in their performance, or may struggle greatly in the aftermath of a prison suicide. Staff may

1 Prison staff may also be involved in internal prison reviews or regional safer custody investigations. These processes are not included here because they are not uniform across England and Wales.

also process involvement in prison suicides differently, with responses ranging from devastation, to seeing the deceased as 'just a number' (Harris, 2015: 172).

Prisoners' family members are likely to have varying understandings of the investigations as they proceed: 'families are not routinely provided with adequate information about the processes that occur following a death' (Harris, 2015: 169). Even if they are informed, they may not comprehend the extent and implications of the process, or struggle to grasp them in their grief. As Stella, the bereaved partner of a prisoner told me, in the immediate aftermath of the death: 'All we were really told was that there would be an investigation by CID[2] and the PPO and wait to hear from us and that was kind of it'. There can also be a lack of clarity for families about the purposes of meetings with investigators, which can aim to both inform and gather information from the family (Shaw and Coles, 2007: 62). Prison staff will also have varying understandings and experiences of these investigations. This chapter cannot claim to speak for all of these different groups, but indicates some individual experiences.

The inquest usually concludes the post-death investigations, but inquest delays can span years rather than months (Harris, 2015: 183) and dates may be set and changed several times (EHRC, 2015b: 32–33). These delays expose all concerned 'to lengthy periods of uncertainty and anxiety' (Liebling, 1998: 69–70). As research in the Republic of Ireland explained: 'prison officers were not only typically the first responders to a death in custody, but also remained connected to the incident in the months, and sometimes years, that followed due to delays in the coronial process' (Barry, 2017: 2). This can feel like a 'highly pressurised' and 'endless' process for staff:

> Governor: 'You need the reports for the Inspector of Prisons, the reports for the Guards, the reports for the

[2] Police Criminal Investigation Department.

> Department, the reports for the Coroner; it's *endless*, it's bloody endless. The administrative end of a death is *endless*. [...] It's highly pressurised, because everyone wants their report *now*. The IPS[3] want their report now, the Inspector wants his reports now, the Press Office want their quotes now; so everyone wants it *now*, you know.' (Barry, 2017: 238)

The potentially lengthy delay before the inquest hearing is interspersed with the police and Ombudsman investigations and clinical review. Whilst each investigation serves a specific purpose, experiencing them in combination may have different effects for the staff and families involved. This has escaped attention. This chapter addresses this gap, collating staff and family experiences of these investigations.

Police

Experiences of the police investigations appear to have been neglected previously – for example, they are not considered in the Harris Review (2015). Although my interviews indicated that the police investigation was generally prompt where there was no evidence of foul play, it can become prolonged. Donna pointed out that "the police are normally in and out if there's no suspicious circumstances". This was supported by Violet and Stella:

> Violet: 'People do make the comparison between how quickly the police investigation happens and the prison ones [...] that was family members who did that. [...] They felt the police were really quick. [...] The prisons [Ombudsman] they felt were much longer.'

---

3 Irish Prison Service.

> Stella (bereaved partner): '[Deceased] got took into hospital on the Friday morning and I think [...] it was the Saturday morning that the CID Officer [...] came in and took a statement. [...] I saw [Deceased] the day that he was arrested. Obviously they wanted a little bit of a statement from me to say [...] what his frame of mind was like and that kind of thing and yeah we didn't really hear much from them after that either. They came round [...] again, I think that was just to ask me a few more questions to be honest, that might have been maybe a month later.'

Alice considered that the police were too unlikely to consider prison suicide cases for prosecution under corporate manslaughter legislation or refer them to the HSE:

> Alice: 'I think more of these cases need to be investigated from a health and safety point of view and that doesn't happen very often [...] these are not viewed in the kind of broader health and safety or indeed corporate manslaughter, which I think is important. [...] Deaths in custody [are] included within the corporate manslaughter legislation but you know we have never seen a prosecution since and very few investigations.'

Although criminal and health and safety investigations are indeed relatively rare, they do occur (see Chapter Two). When prison staff are interviewed regarding involvement in a potential offence, this will be preceded by a caution under the Police and Criminal Evidence Act 1984, which may be stressful in itself and can be followed by a long delay before a charging decision and potential trial.[4] As noted in Chapter Two, Ryan

[4] https://s3-eu-west-2.amazonaws.com/ppo-prod-storage-1g9rkhjhkjmgw/uploads/2014/07/Memorandum_of_Understanding_with_Coroners_-_approved_July_2012.pdf.

Harvey died on 8 May 2015, Joseph Travers was charged on 27 February 2017[5] and acquitted on 30 January 2018.[6] The extent of the police investigation can vary geographically, as explained by Laura: "there are some prisons where the police are very exercised about failings [...] the corporate manslaughter sort of thing slightly muddies the water a bit where the police are concerned." Whilst it is imperative that any potential criminal offences are investigated, extended police investigation of, for example, corporate manslaughter offences delay the Ombudsman and Coroner investigations and are very unlikely to result in a prosecution:

> Laura: 'Initially it was a bit like [...] "we are looking at the actions of this man" and it's just like not going to go anywhere [...] it is so difficult to prove in that context and it would be very difficult to operate if there had been a corporate manslaughter charge against any individual member of staff that wasn't the Governor and even if it was the Governor that would be difficult, you know it would just be really hard to continue working if the corporate manslaughter charge was brought [...] we haven't had one yet.'

More extensive police investigations might increase accountability, but then lead to even longer investigation processes for families and staff, and potentially undermine subsequent Ombudsman and Coroner investigations. Indeed, there is already criticism that Ombudsman investigators are too slow to attend prison: 'often particular documents are not retained and staff accounts are not immediately taken ... often CCTV is destroyed', and 'the more delayed the investigation the more reduced the chances of impact

5 www.bucksfreepress.co.uk/news/national/15120882.Prison_officer_facing_manslaughter_and_misconduct_charges_over_inmate___s_death/.

6 www.bbc.co.uk/news/uk-england-beds-bucks-herts-42878661.

of any resulting recommendations for change' (Harris, 2015: 181). Chapter Two also considered the (in)appropriateness of prosecuting prison staff. The next section examines experiences of the Ombudsman investigation.

Ombudsman

Prison staff experiences of the Ombudsman investigation varied between individuals and with the circumstances of individual deaths:

> Laura: 'Sometimes people find it really positive to speak to [the Ombudsman] and sometimes people are like we haven't really had a chance to sit and think it through [...] You either have people who really resent [the Ombudsman] because they don't think [the Ombudsman] know what [the Ombudsman] are talking about, or you have people who are just desperate for something to be done differently and they want to be part and engage with the learning lessons.'

The Ombudsman investigation takes place in familiar workplace surroundings, rather than in Coroner's court under oath, with the deceased's family potentially in the court. Brian considered that "the ombudsmen are a much, much gentler set of people than coroners [...] it is all about debriefing, about talking things through, getting things off your chest". It was, however, clear that the Ombudsman investigation could become very stressful for staff members, and being audio-recorded could add another layer of anxiety and perceived accountability to the interview:

> Laura: 'I guess you know [the Ombudsman] are recording, you kind of feel like "oh I don't want to say the wrong thing" [...] It's just nerve wracking I guess and people are generally really nervous and often staff are really, really

upset because they have really been involved, with some really complex cases, the staff involvement is really, really intense [...] People just are probably feeling in a very seriously pressurised service, probably just feeling a bit picked on.'

Jeremy: 'The PPO thing actually has more impact I think because it feels more immediate because [the Inspectorate] can follow it up and because the staff involved are going to have been more directly involved, so people are more anxious in a prison about a PPO investigation than they were about a Coroner's hearing. [...] [The Ombudsman investigation is] more immediate and they tend to be more like detailed [...] The PPO people who write the reports and do the conclusions know more about prisons than the Coroner's Court, [...] essentially you are getting an expert who knows a lot about this coming in and looking pretty quickly at what has happened, you are getting some immediate feedback.'

The Ombudsman investigation could also entail significant investment of time and resources for prisoners' families. Family members may feel a responsibility or desire to participate in every stage of the investigation process, but this may disrupt their life significantly:

Stella (bereaved partner): 'The PPO came to visit us. That was a little bit awkward as well because [Deceased]'s sister and mum live in [place] and obviously I'm [about 70 miles away] and they couldn't come to see us all separate, it was easier for them [...] coming up from London to see us all in one place. So that meant I had to get myself [about 70 miles away] to be there on the day [...] we had a meeting with them at [Deceased]'s mum's house and again that was just to tell us, that was quite early on and that was just to

> tell us what their involvement was, what they were going to be doing, anything that they did know so far which at that point was very little, any questions that we had.'

Throughout the investigations, errors and misunderstandings may come to light. These may well be errors rather than deliberate deception, but this can create another burden and sense of 'suspicion' for families to deal with:

> Stella: 'When we got the statements from the PPO, there are some statements from certain officers in the back, we found a lot of them didn't match up and obviously this is when your suspicion starts kicking in, well so and so is saying this but then you have got another person saying this and this time doesn't match up with this time, you know, so I think it's just a natural thing when you go through something like this because when the doubts are there you can't help but, *you need* them answers and when […] you are getting different answers and things don't match up...'

> Prisoners' family member: 'they even lied about where he was found hanging, first it was the window then it was the bed. I knew that I had to fight them to get the truth'. (Harris, 2015: 165)

It will inevitably be challenging for the Ombudsman to provide bereaved families with any sense of satisfaction. Nevertheless, Stella found the process unsatisfying and a "pointless waste of time", despite having invested in it and inconvenienced herself significantly, in part because she felt questions she had raised weren't answered:[7]

7 The Ombudsman collates feedback from all stakeholders. Reports that are useful but based on very small sample sizes are published at www.ppo.gov.uk/document/stakeholder-feedback/.

> Stella: 'The report, I think it took about 12 months. […] We got the draft copy and […] sort of in the small print it said that you could ask any questions in writing regarding the draft. So we did that and we had quite a lot of questions, I mean I wrote a full A4 page list and [Deceased]'s sister also did the same with her different questions, so we had quite a lot between us. And then we waited for the final copy and the answers to our questions which we only got, I would say out of two lists of A4 we probably only got one or two questions answered. We didn't feel it answered our questions. We kind of felt like that had been a pointless waste of time. […] We just got the report and in the report it was just kind of like "well this is the answers to your questions". […] I think what they had done is just answered the ones that they could answer and then any that they couldn't, they'd just not mentioned them.'

The next section examines experiences of the clinical review, which forms part of the Ombudsman investigation.

Clinical review

Clinical reviews are undertaken as part of the Ombudsman investigation into the circumstances surrounding a death, but have received little attention (Harris, 2015: 169). Clinical reviews are commissioned by NHS England/Healthcare Inspectorate Wales and review clinical care according to agreed protocols, including whether referrals to secondary healthcare were made appropriately.[8] Staff experiences of clinical reviews vary because the review takes different forms. Healthcare staff are most likely to be involved in these investigations. The clinical

8 https://s3-eu-west-2.amazonaws.com/ppo-prod-storage-1g9rkhjhkjmgw/uploads/2017/04/PPO-Terms-of-reference-2017.pdf, p 9.

reviewer and the Ombudsman investigator agree the level of the review, choosing level 1, 2 or 3 depending on the circumstances of the case (PPO, 2014b: 2). Level 1 involves only a desk-based review of records, level 2 adds interviews with healthcare staff and level 3 (for complex cases) involves a panel review and may also include interviews with further non-healthcare staff as appropriate (PPO, 2014b: 2). At level 1, staff will likely only experience any recommendations that may be made by the reviewer and filter back to them, but if individuals become aware of an investigation they may have an anxious wait for the findings. At levels 2 and 3, healthcare and potentially further staff who have had significant dealings with the deceased will be interviewed *jointly* by the clinical reviewer and Ombudsman investigator. These interviews will be recorded, the transcripts signed and agreed by the interviewee and annexed to the Ombudsman report, which is provided to the Coroner (PPO, 2014b: 4). Families are routinely not contacted 'as part of the clinical review process, even though the guidance says that they should be' (Harris, 2015: 169). The next section considers the Coroner's inquest, which the Ombudsman report and clinical review inform.

Coroner: "Show some respect, this isn't funny for us"

The inquest brings staff and families (if attending) face to face. Although this can create mutual respect and understanding - for example, prisoners' families have come 'to shake the hands of prison staff by the end of the week' (Ludlow et al, 2015: 60) - it can be difficult for all concerned. Interacting with the deceased's family can be very challenging for prison staff (Ludlow et al, 2015: 60). Families may be further agitated in this scenario given that 'prisons and YOIs were often insensitive in the way in which they engaged with bereaved families immediately after the incident that led to the death' (Harris, 2015: 10; see also Shaw and Coles, 2007: 22-30). Bereaved partner Stella described her distressing experience of coming close to prison staff at the inquest:

> Stella: 'There wasn't a separate family room and that was hard because you sort of hung about in a corridor where the prison officers are […] You can't help but think: well you clearly have got some part in what happened to [Deceased] or else you wouldn't be here today […]. On the very first morning, this is one thing that will *always* stick in my mind […] an officer […] arrived and […] we was sort of hanging about waiting to go in […] and […] one of the Clerks […] was like "oh what are you doing here again", and he went "oh it's my third time here this year". […] I just thought […] *Hello*, we are stood here, […] a grieving family and you are almost bragging about the fact that you are at the Coroner's Court for the third time that year. *You know, show some respect, this isn't funny to us.*'

This also highlights that spates of deaths have occurred in individual prisons. Prison staff (including healthcare staff) and prisoners' family members may all be called to give evidence at inquest and be cross-examined by lawyers and barristers representing different parties (Wright et al, 2012: 94). This can be an intimidating and uncomfortable process for all concerned (Liebling, 1998; Shaw and Coles, 2007; Wright et al, 2012; Barry, 2017: 242–246). Staff are likely to have already given interviews to the Ombudsman but then "relive it twice" at the inquest (Brian). During inquests 'searching questions are asked, emotional scenes may occur, and different participants may come with agendas the inquest is not intended to satisfy' (Liebling, 1998: 69–70). Witnesses may also be concerned about the inquest implicating subsequent civil damages claims or criminal prosecutions (Wright et al, 2012: 94).

The inquest procedures put prison staff 'in the dock' and require them

> to defend each activity, movement, and decision taken during the hours (and sometimes days) leading up to the death … in an unfamiliar, formal territory … their knowledge and understanding of procedures relating to prison suicide would be tested, the quality of their judgments considered, and the extent of their communication with the prisoners addressed. (Liebling, 1998: 72)

As Peay argued (1996: 11), 'subject to this level of analysis, which of us would be likely to be found completely without fault?' Wright et al (2012: 95) have noted the 'burden of scrutiny' placed upon clinicians in secure environments. For all prison staff at inquests, this scrutiny is undertaken with a significant audience:

> Brian: 'Usually you will have legal representation for the family of the deceased, for the prison and for the healthcare provider. So normally you have got three barristers and three barristers assists and healthcare manager, family member and obviously prison manager.'

Of course, these actors can be multiplied if the case implicates further agencies such as police or external healthcare contractors. Against this backdrop, 'any failure to adhere to instructions, communicate effectively with other staff, or to notice and follow up possible indications of suicide risk would become the focus of intense concern from the coroner' (Liebling, 1998: 72-73). A prison manager described the process thus:

> 'It's daunting. You feel you are being personally judged so you can't help but worry about it. You've got five different lawyers all asking questions. Then you've got questions from the coroner and maybe the jury. And none of them know anything about what prison is really like. You come

> out of it feeling blamed and never wanting to go back there again.' (Ludlow et al, 2015: 42).

This investigation and intense questioning 'may occur in the context of inadequate training, lack of confidence among officers about their skills in relation to suicide prevention,[9] staff shortages, overcrowding, inadequate medical support, and sometimes quite serious efforts made by the officer concerned to enlist help for the prisoner during the days before his death' (Liebling, 1998: 72-73). Although some prison staff are prepared, trained and supported for their appearances at inquests (Ludlow et al, 2015: 59), others are not. Furthermore, clinical staff and particularly doctors can qualify with very little knowledge of the Coroner system, as this is not always part of their mandatory training (Wright et al, 2012: 95), despite the high rates of prison suicide. Of course, staff attendance at what can be lengthy investigations and inquests takes them away from their usual duties (Liebling, 1998: 74). Furthermore, prison staff's fear of being called to the Coroner's court can lead to risk aversion and a high number of open ACCT documents, which reduces the quality of ACCT reviews and increases the likelihood of deaths (Ludlow et al, 2015: 43; Shaw, 2017: 14).

The delay between the death and the inquest can affect bereaved families significantly and:

> Alice: 'places a real toll on the family's ability to begin the grieving process and lots of families tell us that they can't begin to grieve until they know the truth. And that process of trying to find out the truth can be not only extremely intrusive but obviously subject to delay.'

9 Chapter One considered deficiencies in staff training with reference to deaths at HMPs Preston and Winchester.

Before the inquest begins, families seeking legal representation may experience difficulties obtaining legal aid:

> Alice: 'You have always got a battle about getting funding, you know, and the inequality of arms and resources is a really serious issue […] it's just not acceptable that the Prison Service can have access to lawyers that we as taxpayers pay for when the family have to battle to try and get kind of funding and have to go through, even if they can get funding […] they have to go through a very intrusive funding application process, that causes a lot of distress within the family dynamic […] it's just inhumane, it really is.'

As noted in Chapter Two, families may also not find out in a timely fashion about the support available to them from the voluntary sector, leaving them 'on their own':

> Stella: 'It was only later that we found out we should have been given a leaflet for INQUEST [the charity] for us to be able to contact them […] but we weren't told about INQUEST at all, it was purely by chance […] 11 months later that we came across INQUEST on the internet […] Which […] wasn't lucky in a sense because obviously it is 11 months that we had kind of lost the chance to prepare and yeah, being on our own but it was lucky in one sense […] we only had 12 months to seek legal representation for the actual inquest itself and so it's through speaking to INQUEST then that they informed us and quickly got us a solicitor.'
> Interviewer: 'So you were just left with nothing for 11 months?'
> Stella: 'Basically yeah.'

Once the inquest begins, families must 'wrestle with formality, direction by the coroner, lack of information, and the exposure to the outcome of a series of investigations that they have no power to influence' (Liebling, 1998: 73). Stella illustrated this:

> Stella: 'In that setting you don't know what, you are kind of told be quiet and if you have got owt to ask your barrister you have got to whisper it or ask when you are on the break [...] you are literally like spectators and it feels kind of like watching a show but these people are all discussing what happened to your loved one and yet you feel like you are not involved.'

Inquests can be single day (Liebling, 1998: 74) or last far longer. Stella's family had over a "two-year wait" before a "five-week inquest" which "had quite a lot of people to give evidence [...] because there was a lot to his case". This length of inquest appears to be atypical,[10] but nevertheless:

> Stella: "It was every day, obviously, apart from weekends and that was [...] like an hour journey every morning to be there for 9:00 and it was tiring and [...] I had my children [also the deceased's children] as well, I wasn't getting home until sort of 6:00, 6:30 and I was setting off before they had even left for school. So for that five-week period that was really tiring and obviously just sat in inquest all day, you know, and it's all solicitors, barristers, talk going on, you know, it's mentally and physically draining.'

Again, the inquest process often throws up errors or misunderstandings as it unfolds:

10 Sean Rigg died after police contact in 2008 and had a seven-week inquest which began four years after his death (Baker, 2016: 7, 82).

> Alice: 'Recent poor practice has been, for example, a family not having a suicide letter disclosed […] they only discovered it at the inquest, by which time they had conducted a funeral and it went against everything that the woman had put in her letter. So you still get kind of pretty shocking experiences like that.'

Stella also experienced errors that "kept nagging on" her mind for a long time "through the two-year wait" and were ultimately exposed at the inquest. Shortly before his death, her partner was transferred to another prison. Throughout the investigation, the deceased's family were led to believe that he was fine when he got on the transfer bus, but during an hour's bus ride he commenced a dirty protest and had to be taken off the bus by "five prison officers in full riot gear", then being "put into segregation for punishment", where he hanged himself "two days later". Stella and the deceased's family were "told that [Deceased] was fine until he got to the other prison. There were no problems […] they couldn't give us any proof that he was fine. There was no CCTV evidence of him getting on the bus". They were informed that the deceased was on the bus alone, so there were no other witnesses. Stella explained:

> 'It never made sense to me, literally from day one and […] on our very first meeting with the PPO that was one of my questions to them, were there any other prisoners on the bus that were potential witnesses? And they said we will […] find out for you and their answer […] was [Deceased] was on the bus on his own. And then I asked the CID […] surely there must be some sort of log. A gate log, you know, something like that […] he also said no [Deceased] was on the bus on his own and it never ever from day one rung true. […] I kept coming up with the same answer wherever I turned, he was on the bus on his own. And then at the inquest two years later, it came out,

> kind of purely accidental through someone's evidence that [Deceased] wasn't on the bus on his own and this is two years later, after being told by PPO and CID. […] The Coroner said at that stage of the inquest it was too late to try and find those people because it meant […] stopping the inquest and […] somebody would have to try and find them because they might no longer be in prison. […] We weren't allowed to know the names of those prisoners. That was classed as confidential. […] So in our minds that is another […] four or five other prisoners that were potential witnesses.'

This was extremely significant to Stella, who said:

> 'I'll never believe that he just got on that bus all fine […] and suddenly he just lost his mind within an hour, you know to the point that he did something that was completely, totally and utterly out of character. […] Those other prisoners, either way […] it might have been what we believe that he would have been kicking off and that he didn't go of his own free will kind of thing onto the bus […] or they might have agreed with the prison. […] From the beginning that's all we asked, whether we liked it or not, we just wanted the truth. How can you ever have closure without all the answers? […] We were hoping when it came to the inquest that that is what the inquest is for, it's a fact finding exercise and you kind of hope that when you go there, you are going to get all your answers and that's it […] you are going to get your answers finally and you are going to be able to move on and you are going to be able to do your grieving […] and start looking forward but it didn't work like that for us because we still didn't get the answers. We still haven't got the answers to this day.'

As such, having potentially invested significant time, energy and resources into the investigative process, families may receive unsatisfactory outcomes. Although the investigative process is certainly challenged to ameliorate their loss, clearly some outcomes simply are not acceptable:

> Family: 'After the inquest we received a one line letter from [the governor] saying he was sorry for our loss. We received this one month after the inquest where the jury found that "neglect" contributed to [his] death. I was disgusted. It was an insult, a waste of paper!' (Harris, 2015: 165)

After a five-week inquest into the death of Stella's partner, the Coroner made a PFD report, but despite the statutory requirement that the prison respond within 56 days, a response was not made:

> Stella: 'We were kind of told what happens with the recommendations is they get sent to the prison, the prison has to follow them up, or if they are not going to follow them up say why they are not following up etc etc, Which for us was good because that is what we wanted ultimately [...]. We wanted to spare this happening to other families. That was our main, you know – aside from getting answers for [Deceased] and answers for ourselves, it was to stop this happening again. So those recommendations were made and we were told we'd hear from the prison [...]. That was in October 2015 and still to this day (February 2017) we haven't heard a word. [...] A worker at INQUEST [...] actually contacted the prison for us about, I don't know maybe six months ago now [...] to basically ask why have the family not yet received a response to the recommendations and still we've heard nothing. We have literally had no contact at all with that prison.'

During our interview, I advised Stella that the prison were obliged to respond and my understanding is that she then followed up via INQUEST again, ultimately receiving a response from HMPPS in mid-2017 with apologies for 'an administrative error' having delayed their response.

Discussion

The long, multifaceted investigations after prison suicides can be significant for all concerned. They can lead to life-saving changes to policy and practice, although this should not be taken for granted as a probable outcome. Sometimes families are informed about changes made in response to the death of their relative:

> One family described how they found comfort in knowing that ligature points have been removed. One family member described the value of knowing that 'two suicides had been prevented in the prison where my son died because of changes made after his death'. Another took similar comfort, saying 'I waited three years for someone to tell me he didn't die for nothing'.[11] (Harris, 2015: 170)

The Ombudsman and Coroner clearly have a difficult task, examining the actions of what can be complex individuals, with complex histories, in complicated and imperfect custodial environments. Both may also confront some stakeholders' desires or expectations that their investigation might "find an individual that should have done something differently and hang them out to dry, you know or somehow heal what is just the most devastating loss, which we can't" (Laura).

[11] But see Chapter Two regarding the sometimes unhelpful discourse of 'lesson learning' and prisoners dying for some manufactured purpose.

Nevertheless, the potential *burden of these investigations on families and staff* should not be underestimated. As Brian pointed out, giving interviews to the Ombudsman and the Coroner can lead to prison staff reliving potentially traumatic events twice and this may also apply to families. These investigations hold potential for secondary victimisation of families (Shapland et al, 1985), who may be vulnerable and stigmatised due to the death and indeed before the death (Laxminarayan, 2013). Although positive experience of investigations can be supportive for families, their ability to cope may be lessened by detrimental experiences (Laxminarayan, 2013; Harris, 2015: 167).

These investigations are also far from guaranteed to stimulate reform: 'for thirty years INQUEST has monitored inquests into deaths in custody. One of the striking features of this work has been our repeated experience of attending inquest after inquest where the same issues are identified as possibly contributing to the death' (Coles and Shaw, 2012: 1). Peay (1996: 30) has argued, in the context of public inquiries after homicide, that detriment to those 'awaiting and undergoing the process … can only be weighed against the effectiveness of … conclusions and recommendations'. However, the public hearing of the case and recording of the circumstances can also be important and indeed are required by Article 2.

It is possible that available evidence about the effectiveness of investigations is skewed to highlight failures, such that instances of successful learning are unreported: 'every life lost in prison is a tragedy. Every life saved goes virtually unnoticed' (Shaw, 2017: 3). If lesson learning fails, the outcome can be, as Dave phrased it: "the same death occurring in the same way in the same prison". This is of course highlighted by the investigations, which do not occur if the processes lead to changes in policy or practice that save lives. Nevertheless, Stella's experience led me to seriously question the fairness of involving a family in a five-week inquest process, after Ombudsman and police investigations, resulting in a PFD report that the prison did not respond to for well over a year, and only then after being followed up twice. Stella's is an extreme case and the families are not obliged to participate in any of the investigations, although they may feel a responsibility to the deceased or obligation to participate to help prevent future deaths.

Although the police, Ombudsman and Coroner all have different remits and in some senses comprise an evolving process of investigation, it is questionable whether all bodies need to be involved. Whilst Angiolini (2017) and others have called for a single body to coordinate lesson learning (see Chapter Two), there has been less attention given to coordinated investigation, which could benefit families and staff by reducing the burden of investigations. Nevertheless, such refinement could also compromise the independence and timeliness of investigations and further divert attention from systemic and structural issues implicated in prison suicides.

Given the already substantial burden of investigations, I am cautious[12] about Harris' (2015: 169) recommendation that families should be contacted as part of the clinical review 'in order to better support families and ensure that lessons are more effectively learned'. The appended analysis of clinical reviews also recommended that 'the family should be given access to the findings prior to publication for comments' and that the lead clinical reviewer should have 'expertise in facilitating family involvement' (Maganty et al, 2015: 21). It is essential that families are involved in post-death investigations under Article 2, but recommendations should be tempered by experiential understandings of what families and staff go through, the extended periods of time that they are already caught up in

[12] Public service regulation has been characterised as 'an "industry" which seemed to have grown topsy-like' (Hood et al, 1999: 5), and prison regulation as 'successive responses to *ad hoc* inquiries, shaped by particular incidents or crises to which Home Secretaries felt obliged to respond' (Hood et al, 1999: 120) which have 'frequently added new parts to the oversight system but seldom took anything away' (Hood et al, 1999: 119).

investigations, and the (unrealistic) belief that their participation in an inquest might save lives:

> Stella: 'I actually found out from INQUEST that there had been 12 other deaths since [Deceased], just in [single prison] alone and obviously at that point last year he had only been gone three years. Twelve since [Deceased] in three years. […] Everyone we hear about, it's like a kick in the teeth for us all over again and I think all families would tell you the same to be honest. […] Clearly that speaks for itself, things aren't getting better and clearly the recommendations, either they are not being adhered to or something's not right because it's getting worse. That is what it is meant to be for, you know, so that lessons can be learned, […] deaths can be prevented.'

Given the unclear relationship between the findings of investigations and on-the-ground changes, it is important that families have access to full, impartial information about the investigations and their potential, such that they can make an informed decision regarding if and how to participate, and be supported through this complex, lengthy series of investigations. I agree that it is unacceptable that 'the burden of providing basic information about the inquest system is currently placed on the voluntary sector' (Shaw and Coles 2007: 41). Indeed, families have 'explained how painful it is to have to tell the story again and again and how anxious it can make them worrying about what the advisor might think about them because their relative died in custody' (Shaw and Coles, 2007: 40). Currently, the prison Family Liaison Officer is the family's main point of contact from when news of the death is broken to them (Harris, 2015: 167). These officers have a conflicting role: having contact with the prisoners' family in the early days following a death but then potentially supporting prison staff at the inquest or giving evidence themselves (Harris, 2015: 168). *Having any member of prison staff advising the family is problematic.*

The Ministry of Justice funds the charity Victim Support to deliver a Homicide Service[13] to bereaved families. A homicide case worker helps people to navigate and know what to expect from the criminal justice system and provides someone independent to talk to and assist with practical needs.[14] There is a *clear need for the MoJ to fund such a service for the families of those who die in prison.* As Baker (2016: 205) notes with reference to deaths after police contact: 'people die, they do not return. They leave behind families and friends who are grief stricken because of the death, and often doubly traumatised because they feel the accountability process does not construct legitimate outcomes'. Furthermore, the processes of investigation themselves can have lasting effects on bereaved families. Chapter One noted that Sean Plumstead's mother heard about the delay in answering his cell bell at the inquest and would 'forever wonder about what might have happened had staff got to Sean within the time they were supposed to'.[15] This chapter has detailed how bereaved partner Stella hoped the inquest would mean she got "answers finally", enabling her to move on and grieve. Unfortunately, "it didn't work like that for us because we still didn't get the answers. We still haven't got the answers to this day". An adequately resourced specialist service for bereaved families would go some way towards reducing the degree of this double and enduring trauma.

I am also *uneasy about the degree of scrutiny individual staff* come under from the Ombudsman and Coroner. An oft-repeated Ombudsman recommendation is that 'staff place too much emphasis on how a prisoner seems during their brief contact',

13 www.gov.uk/government/publications/moj-grant-agreement-with-victim-support-to-operate-the-national-homicide-service.

14 www.victimsupport.org.uk/more-us/why-choose-us/specialist-services/homicide-service.

15 www.theguardian.com/society/2017/oct/19/hmp-winchester-inmate-staff-suicide-sean-plumstead.

recommending that staff 'should make a considered, objective evaluation of all other risk factors for suicide and self-harm and document their evaluation' (PPO, 2017a: 23). Yet Chapter Two described how prison staff are now set up to fail in following ACCT procedures: the Prison Service Instructions and Orders protect the MoJ but do not enable staff to protect prisoners. Furthermore, the situation in practice may be frenzied. For example, 'one or two members of healthcare staff often have to complete extremely high numbers of prisoners' initial assessments in a short space of time (usually between 12 mid-day and 8 pm following the court sessions and sentencing process) making it almost impossible to establish any detail' (McKenzie, 2014: 2–3). One prison officer described Reception as 'an inherently dehumanising sausage factory' (Ludlow et al, 2015: 28). Clearly, staff and governors have some agency to create material and cultural differences in their individual prisons (Ludlow et al, 2015: 28) and standards of accountability in closed penal institutions must be high. Staff and governors have some agency and influence, but it is limited:

> 'Decisions have been made by successive politicians about what happens in prisons and they have not been held accountable. [...] If you decide to cut staff, [...] people die as a consequence. If you decide to [...] cram everybody into fetid cells that they are sharing with a toilet and cockroaches, their mental health will deteriorate and people will die as a consequence. [...] It is not inadvertent. [...] Politicians of all parties have made decisions that they were warned at the time would cause overcrowding, [...] would damage people's mental health and resilience. [...] I would point in particular to [Grayling's] decisions [...] to cut staff, cut budgets, close prisons, cram people into fewer prisons and destroy the community sentence structure. [...] Successive Justice Secretaries have led us down the path

> to where we are today.' (Frances Crook's evidence to the Joint Committee on Human Rights, 2017b)

When these conditions have implications such as 'medical and mental health appointments being missed because there are not sufficient staff available to escort the patient' (Harris, 2015: 10) and result in prisoner deaths, it is individual members of staff who are scrutinised. As such, both Ombudsman and Coroner recommendations may justifiably be seen by prison staff as 'too aspirational' (Ludlow et al, 2015: 38), or 'inappropriate, unrealistic or a reflection of being poorly informed about the 'realities' of prison life' (Ludlow et al, 2015: 58). Brian stated: "I do kind of wonder that if you have got so many repeat recommendations what are you doing" and mused that perhaps:

> 'the person who is producing the report inevitably feels the compulsion to make recommendations at the end of it and it is pretty dull to produce a report that just says "yeah the prison did everything right". [...] You know if you have got someone who is dead the family want to see something change and want to see that recommendations have been made to stop it from happening again to somebody else and that's I guess there must be a compulsion by the PPO investigators to say actually to the family, look we have recommended that this changes and that can be difficult for the families I feel because they then are led into this position of thinking well if that was different then actually.'

I disagree with Brian as I have read numerous Ombudsman reports where no recommendations are made and have seen acknowledgements such as 'it is very difficult to prevent someone who has made a determined decision to kill themselves from carrying that out and I do not consider that prison staff could have predicted or prevented Mr Murphy's actions'.[16] However, the large proportion of repeated Ombudsman and Coroner recommendations indicate that prison staff are unable to operate how overseers expect them to, that prison staff do not care about their stigmatised prisoner charges (see Chapter One), or that the recommendations are worthless and do not facilitate change. There may be some truth in all of these, but it is clear that prison staff cannot now operate ACCT as prescribed in the Prison Service Instruction (Ludlow et al, 2015: 40; Shaw, 2017: 36). As such, it is unfair that inquest proceedings can expose prison staff 'to feelings of individual accountability in a way that is potentially damaging' (Liebling, 1998: 70) when they have some, but limited ability to alter prison conditions. At inquests, 'shortcoming in policy or staff training as to the requirements of the policy may become exposed … families often find this process traumatic and frustrating. Yet it is officers who feel the impact of their distress' (Liebling, 1998: 73). Some sensible recommendations have been made regarding training staff for inquests (Wright et al, 2012: 94). However, these experiential improvements should not negate the need for *accountability of political decision makers*. HMPPS, Ministers and Secretaries of State may receive a PFD report and, as Chapter Two demonstrated, HMPPS will most likely respond for all three, but receiving a letter is in no way comparable to being cross-examined under oath in a court. Harris (2015: 57) notes that the Minister for Prisons 'needs to feel responsible for each life in custody, and should respond to each death', with which I firmly agree, although I would argue that the Secretary of State should be designated. If the Minister or Secretary was called as a witness to every inquest for a prisoner's self-inflicted death, for example

[16] https://s3-eu-west-2.amazonaws.com/ppo-dev-storage-4dvljl6iqfyh/uploads/2016/03/L052-15-Death-of-Mr-Anthony-Murphy-Norwich-29-05-2015-SID-51-60.pdf.

in prisons known to be understaffed, they would very quickly wish to reduce numbers.

This chapter has explored prison staff and prisoners' families' experiences of the full complement of post-prison suicide investigations. It has highlighted the burden that these investigations can impose on bereaved familied and prison staff, raised concerns about the degree of scrutiny to which prison staff can be subjected given their limited agency, noted the unclear relationship between the findings of post-suicide investigations and suicide prevention and restated the need for accountability of political decision makers. A publicly resourced independent support service for bereaved families was suggested. The next chapter explores *what post-suicide investigations achieve.*

4

Prison oversight

Introduction

This book has examined post-prison suicide oversight mechanisms, contributing to public bureaucracy oversight scholarship. The first analysis of post-prison suicide investigations under Article 2 and the NPM has been provided using the case study of England and Wales. England and Wales has a substantial prison monitoring and post-death investigations framework, yet experienced record numbers of prison suicides in 2016 following swingeing staff cuts. Chapter One detailed the global importance of analysing prison suicide investigations, emphasising that 'manipulative' prisoner behaviour can be lethal and illustrating the underappreciated roles of suicidogenic discourses, institutional apathy and prisoner stigmatisation in suicide prevention.

Chapter Two explored *how* post-suicide investigations operate in England and Wales, describing the police, Ombudsman and Coroner investigations that usually form the Article 2-compliant investigation, and considering potential criminal prosecutions and HSE activity. It illustrated these investigations through the 2013–2016 suicide cluster at HMP Woodhill, arguing that existing investigations provide no shortage of vigorous critique, although there is a problematic lag between the death and subsequent findings. Chapter Two identified limitations in Article 2, which does not require that lessons produced by post-death investigations be applied, and does not direct accountability towards those with capacity to implement said lessons, who are primarily senior politicians. Chapter Two challenged the discourse of lesson learning, which can *manufacture mystery* around what are often entirely manifest and previously identified issues, and may obfuscate the contribution of political decisions to issues. Chapter Three considered how the full complement of post-suicide investigations *are experienced*, highlighting the *burden that these investigations can impose* on bereaved families and prison staff. It raised concerns about the degree of scrutiny to which prison staff can be subjected, given their limited agency and training, and recommended a state-resourced independent support service for bereaved families. This chapter explores *what post-suicide investigations achieve*, which is linked to broader prison oversight.

Prison oversight is an important 'counterweight to potential abuse of the special powers of the state' (Hood et al, 1999: 116) and there is a complex, 'wide and overlapping field of bodies with inspection or regulatory powers within and across criminal justice' (Owers, 2010: 239). Nevertheless, there is a 'striking' lack of research on prison oversight (Seddon, 2010: 279). This fits the general pattern of interest in the oversight of business and privatised utilities, leaving public bureaucracy oversight 'imperfectly mapped' (Hood et al, 1999: 3). This chapter is structured using the three elements of oversight mechanisms: directors, detectors and effectors (Stirton and Lodge, 2001). *Directors* are means for establishing the purposes of the system, *detectors* are instruments through which data about a situation are passed to the centre of control and *effectors* are instruments for effecting change in the state of the world, feeding instructions from the centre of control (Stirton and Lodge, 2001: 483–484). My argument is that prisons have no shortage of directors and detectors, but very limited effectors, both in relation to prison suicide and in general (Hood et al, 1999).

Regarding directors, prison staff have an embarrassment of policies they should follow, pertaining to all aspects of prison life (including the management of suicide and self-harm). This guidance is difficult to follow and out of date in places, and is also not underpinned by a primary purpose or prioritised series of purposes, but instead by a series of aims which may contradict each other. Contradicting aims are implicated in some suicides. Post-suicide investigations create yet another set of directors produced by multiple bodies. There are also multiple detectors, including the post-death Ombudsman and Coroner investigations and, more generally, internal prison and Prison Service monitoring; oversight by Controllers in private prisons; potential prison inspections by the Inspectorate, Independent Monitoring Boards (IMBs), Environmental Health Officers and HSE inspectors; systemic oversight by the European Committee for the Prevention of Torture, EHRC, Treasury and National Audit Office (NAO). Although there are benefits associated with having multiple detectors from different sectors, this also serves to constrain the remits of each overseer, deprioritise their recommendations, obfuscate pathways to improvement (such as the need to avoid criminalisation of and expedite hospital transfers for those prisoners with severe mental health problems) and constrain remedial action (as seen when prison staffing was increased in response to deteriorating conditions, contrary to Treasury guidelines).

Effectors are limited, but this should not dissuade existing prison overseers from repeatedly targeting critique at those who can effect systemic change. Overseers could target government far more succinctly, repeatedly and vigorously. If overseers do not do this, it lets government off the hook for prison conditions that are largely of their making and penalises prison staff for conditions that can be beyond their control. Given the legitimising effects of prison oversight, overseers have a *responsibility* to speak truth to politicians, which (arguably) outweighs any constraints in their remits. In addition to directors, detectors and effectors, there is scope for overseers to provide far more praise to prison staff, seeking to reinforce and spread examples of good practice.

I suggest that the Ombudsman and Inspectorate could trial standalone 'good practice' documents.

Overall, it is difficult to establish the merit of post-death investigations. Their failures are highlighted but their successes are not (see Chapter Three). My position is that prison overseers in England and Wales *are* more than legitimising functions that shore up state activity, but that they could achieve significantly more by targeting the government succinctly, repeatedly and robustly. However, my argument could be very different if my fieldwork had been undertaken during a less acute prisons crisis. In such circumstances, potential staff and institutional stigmatisation of prisoners (see Chapter One) may be more telling, requiring different recommendations for oversight. I conclude by arguing that there is value in post-suicide investigations, referring to the investigations which followed the deaths of Dean Saunders and Sarah Reed. I suggest that it is all our responsibility to argue that the situations in which Dean Saunders and Sarah Reed died were not aberrations, but *foreseeable outcomes of marooning very sick people in prison.*

Prison directors

The Prison Rules 1999 comprise 85 principal items and were set by then Home Secretary Jack Straw under his rule-making powers in section 47 of the Prison Act 1952. The Prison Rules govern how prisons are run and regulate regime aspects such as physical welfare and discipline. These Rules are 'not "actionable", in that they cannot in any circumstances give rise to a claim for breach of statutory duty', although the Human Rights Act 1998 applies 'in full force to the Rules, and to all action taken under them' (Owen and Macdonald, 2015: 22). The broad canvas of the Prison Rules is filled in by the administrative guidance and directions of Prison Service Orders and Prison Service Instructions (Owen and Macdonald, 2015:

25).[1] As explained in Chapters One and Two, prison suicide prevention processes are set out in the 70-page Prison Service Instruction 64/2011, with reference to 17 further associated Orders and Instructions. The *plethora of Prison Service Orders and Instructions might of course be strategic*: to legitimise prisons and their problematic practices and to obfuscate accountability for deaths (Hancock and Liebling, 2013), but they fail to provide simple directions for staff. Local assessment tools and policies may also exist for individual establishments, for example in relation to suicide prevention and incident response (PPO, 2017a: 23). Of course, practice often differs from that stated in national and local policies.[2] Despite containing 'massive detail relevant to the conduct of daily life in prison', Prison Service Orders and Instructions 'have no legislative authority', being no more than non-statutory guidance to those managing prisons (Owen and Macdonald, 2015: 26).

Nevertheless, as demonstrated by the Woodhill judicial review judgment and HMPPS's responses to coroners' PFD reports described in Chapter Two, the mere existence of this non-statutory guidance absolves the MoJ of much responsibility for prison suicides, despite the impossibility of prison staff knowing about and being able to implement all of the Orders and Instructions:

> Dave:[3] 'Prison Service Instructions [...] they are about this high... [...] There's a lot of good stuff in them but there's no way that they can all be implemented and indeed [...] the MoJ doesn't actually have any means for

[1] Orders and Instructions resulted from the Woodcock Report into the escape of six prisoners from HMP Whitemoor in 1994 (Home Office, 1994: 94).

[2] See *R (Hamilton-Jackson)* v *Assistant Coroner for Mid Kent and Medway* [2016] EWHC 1796 (Admin).

[3] Quotations throughout this chapter are from representatives of different bodies overseeing post-prison suicide investigations.

telling whether people are following […] Instructions, so what they were saying was "yes this is fine we are doing this already it is in Prison Service Instructions", which didn't quite meet the point because we had only made the recommendation, for example about improved communications, because it wasn't working.'

Violet: 'We disseminated [our findings] as widely as we could. We […] received a government response to that, which perhaps wasn't quite as exercised in the MoJ response as it was in fact the others […] you know there was a sense of "oh well we have done all of this" and we are not completely convinced that's the case.'

In addition to the plethora of Prison Service Orders and Instructions, the Inspectorate sets its own criteria for inspections, to 'ensure transparency and independence', and these are referenced against international human rights standards (HMIP, 2017: 9). The Inspectorate uses over 500 criteria defining best practice in all aspects of prison life, grouped under four key expectations (Owers, 2010: 251):

- Safety – prisoners, particularly the most vulnerable, are held safely
- Respect – prisoners are treated with respect for their human dignity
- Purposeful activity – prisoners are able, and expected, to engage in activity that is likely to benefit them
- Resettlement – prisoners are prepared for their release back into the community and effectively helped to reduce the likelihood of reoffending. (HMIP, 2017: 1)

The Inspectorate's expectations exist in addition to the varying mission statements of statutory bodies. Rule 3 of the Prison Rules 1999 provides the Prison Service mission statement: 'the purpose of the training and treatment of convicted prisoners shall be to encourage and assist them to lead a good and useful life'. The MoJ website alternatively states: 'We work to ensure that sentences are served and offenders are encouraged to turn their lives around and become law-abiding citizens' and sets a strategic priority of delivering 'a prison and probation service that reforms offenders'.[4] HMPPS is 'here to prevent victims by changing lives. We work with our partners to carry out the sentences given by the courts, either in custody or the community. We reduce reoffending by rehabilitating the people in our care through education and employment'.[5] Amidst this context of multiple directors, the 2016 Prison Safety and Reform White Paper quite rightly identified the need 'to establish an overarching statutory purpose of the prison, with a clear vision of what it is there to achieve' (MoJ, 2016: 9). The statutory purpose is subject to the passage of legislation (MoJ, 2016: 9), which was delayed by the 2017 general election, but thus far is:

> Prisons exist to deprive people of their liberty and so punish them for crimes they have committed. However, the time people spend in prison is an important opportunity to prevent them going on to commit further crimes on release. To achieve that, there are four purposes that prisons need to deliver well:
>
> - protect the public;
> - maintain safety and order;
> - reform offenders to prevent more crimes from being committed; and
> - prepare prisoners for life outside the prison. (MoJ, 2016: 20)

4 www.gov.uk/government/organisations/ministry-of-justice/about.

5 www.gov.uk/government/organisations/her-majestys-prison-and-probation-service/about.

The Commons Justice Select Committee (House of Commons, 2017: 14) identified difficulties with these multiple purposes, advising that the MoJ 'must provide clarity both to governors and to the public about how it intends to weight indicators of performance, including which it sees as of primary importance'. Disappointingly, the government responded 'any weightings introduced for new measures, will reflect the priorities set out in the Prison Safety and Reform White Paper' (House of Commons, 2017: 14). This response failed to engage with the slippage between one clear statutory purpose and *multiple, likely contradictory statutory purposes* unless there is obvious prioritisation.

It is essential to clarify the primacy of stated purposes, the relationships between them, and what is to be done when purposes are in conflict (Zedner, 2004: 257). For example, after escapes from HMPs Whitemoor and Parkhurst in 1994–1995 there was a political commitment to security. Home Secretary Michael Howard emphasised that the first duty of the Prison Service was to keep prisoners in secure custody, and then Director General of the Prison Service told all governing governors that the top three Prison Service priorities were security, security and security (Resodihardjo, 2009). The Prison Service then increased emphasis on security measures and procedures, which undermined rehabilitative programmes such as community work projects (HMIP, 1995: 1). This illustrates how objectives such as training, turning lives around, reform, education and employment can so easily be displaced by fluctuating security concerns.

Contradictions between prison priorities were illustrated by a death at HMP Haverigg on 9 May 2014. On 29 March 2014, this prisoner moved into a new cell. When it was searched later that day officers 'found part of a screwdriver and some items associated with drug taking. The man was charged with a disciplinary offence for possession of these items. (It was later accepted that the items had been left behind by the previous occupant of the cell and the charge was dismissed)' (PPO,

2015b: 12). On 8 May, the man's application to attend a family day at the prison was refused but he was not told the reason (PPO, 2015b: 13). He was upset about this as he had hoped to spend time with his new baby daughter, whom he had not yet met (PPO, 2015b: 3, 9). Although the charge regarding the screwdriver and drug equipment had been dismissed, 'there was still a negative comment about this on his record and this had led to him being refused permission to attend the family day' (PPO, 2015b: 14). Here, concern with safety and order had (in this case unjustly) overridden the need to prepare prisoners for life outside the prison through a family day.

Post-death investigations themselves create yet another set of directors from different bodies, which may contain conflicting injunctions (see also Zedner, 2004: 257). Whilst there is value in evaluating the circumstances of each death, publishing them and producing action plans to address recommendations made, this can also create further confusion. As highlighted by the Zahid Mubarek Inquiry:

> You lose sight of the things you have to do if they are duplicated in many places. And to the extent that they contain overlapping recommendations, it may be difficult to know exactly what you are being asked to do. … The detailed action plans the Prison Service has grown to expect – can result in an establishment's management team not looking at the bigger picture. They can become so concerned about addressing each of the many action points that they lose sight of the wider strategic approach which may be necessary to resolve the establishment's underlying problems. (House of Commons, 2006: 433–434)

Because prisons deprive people of their liberty, oversight is quite correct. Relatively 'independent'[6] evaluation of prison

[6] Chapter Two considers the quasi-independent nature of these bodies.

suicides by the Ombudsman, Coroner and Inspectorate and publication of their reports can be a strength, not least in counteracting sanitised state accounts produced with minimal scrutiny (Hancock and Liebling, 2013) and reducing the risks of stagnation or capture in the oversight regimes[7] (Hood et al, 1999: 138). However, the involvement of multiple bodies increases the burden of investigation (see Chapter Three), further obfuscates the already confused directors for prisons and is not automatically a safeguard against failure. An example from another field is the finding that serious failings at the Mid Staffordshire NHS Foundation Trust between 2005 and 2009 led to 'appalling suffering of many patients', despite 'a plethora of agencies, scrutiny groups, commissioners, regulators and professional bodies, all of whom might have been expected by patients and the public to detect and do something effective to remedy non-compliance with acceptable standards of care' (House of Commons, 2013: 3).

Prison detectors

The post-suicide Ombudsman and Coroner investigations and follow-up from the Inspectorate usually produce many recommendations, in addition to the extensive Prison Service Orders and Instructions. The scale of recommendations that prison governors are responsible for implementing is vast. This scale of recommendations can dilute the potency of calls for reform:

[7] Although I did not come across cases of disagreement between overseers in the prison context, in policing jury inquest verdicts have differed considerably from the Independent Police Complaints Commission's reports (which is similar to the PPO), for example in the death of Sean Rigg (Baker, 2016).

> Jeremy: 'If you're actually a Prison Governor you might have literally hundreds of recommendations you are supposed to be dealing with [...] now actually I think that served to almost like de-prioritise.'[8]

The sheer number of regulators could also (be perceived to) tightly constrain each regulator's remit, encouraging overseers to focus on the pathology or vulnerability of the deceased individuals and deflecting attention from wider systemic, cultural, operational and policy issues that have a direct bearing on prisoner well-being and levels of distress (Scraton and Chadwick, 1987; Razack, 2015; Gooch, 2016):

> Violet: 'I like to think that we helped, you know, persuade government of the need for a different approach to prisons and penal care. You know what we never did, you call it going upstream, we never looked at whether those people should be in prison in the first place, we didn't say we think there are people being held in prisons who shouldn't be there. In our progress report I think we said quite strongly that we weren't able to make those kind of, you know that wasn't within our remit.'

> Joanne: 'Nobody's looking at why people are in prison in the first place. It isn't the Coroner or PPO's fault but it is nobody's remit to check, nobody's saying should this person have been in prison in the first place? We put a lot of people in prison and there's nobody looking at whether that is reasonable. [...] This is the bit of the system not getting critiqued. [...] Nobody is drawing it all together to say systemically we have a problem.'

8 Angiolini (2017: 230) also notes the potential 'fatigue' for custody and healthcare staff 'if they are being given numerous lessons to digest from a variety of sources'.

Such systemic issues were pointed out in the Ombudsman's 2016 annual report. Despite it being beyond their remit 'to make judgements on the resourcing of prisons', they reported that:

> staff at all levels are struggling to manage the detailed and prescribed levels of interaction, recording and evaluation set out in the ACCT process. They are often managing numerous prisoners on busy and demanding wings, while at the same time, managers are focused on attempting to deliver the broader prison regime. (PPO, 2017a: 25)

Although I generally agree that the Ombudsman and Coroner focus on procedural requirements to the detriment of questioning the appropriateness of prison for prisoners (for example, Scraton and Chadwick, 1986), they are not entirely inattentive to the latter, although perhaps only in extreme cases.[9] The Ombudsman has noted, for example:

- 'I have concerns about the boy's location in a young offender institution in the first place' (re the 2012 death of a boy imprisoned at Cookham Wood[10]).
- 'Mr Saunders was acutely mentally ill and all those involved in his care agreed that prison was not an appropriate place for him. Yet the systems designed to divert him from prison did not operate effectively. I am also concerned that there appears to have been some confusion at Chelmsford about

---

9 For example, the Ombudsman made no comment about the remanding of Mr Tony Legge into HMP Chelmsford where he killed himself, charged with stealing meat from a petrol station. https://s3-eu-west-2.amazonaws.com/ppo-prod-storage-1g9rkhjhkjmgw/uploads/2016/01/K243-15-Death-of-Mr-Tony-Legge-in-hospital-Chelmsford-03-03-2015-SID-22-30.pdf.

10 https://s3-eu-west-2.amazonaws.com/ppo-prod-storage-1g9rkhjhkjmgw/uploads/2014/12/G207-12-Death-of-a-boy-in-hospital-Cookham-Wood-25-01-2012-SID-14-17.pdf, p 3.

> the process for transferring mentally ill prisoners to hospital, which meant that an opportunity to transfer Mr Saunders in December was missed. Sadly, the Criminal Justice System did too little to protect this very vulnerable man' (re Dean Saunders, PPO, 2016a: i).

Dean Saunders' PFD report also directed NHS England to consider 'whether the transfer of individuals such as Dean to prison is indeed 'best practice', taking into account the consequent delay in transfer and the suitability of the prison environment for mentally disordered individuals'.[11] The NHS England reply did not engage with the substantive issue of too few secure hospital beds and limited community services, but noted that 'the decision to remand Mr Saunders to HMP Chelmsford was made by Basildon Magistrate's Court'.[12]

Indeed, the European Committee for the Prevention of Torture has been very clear on the importance of reducing the UK prison population.[13] The Committee visited the UK from 30 March to 12 April 2016, reviewing YOI Cookham Wood, HMP&YOI Doncaster and HMP Pentonville, amongst broader detention facilities (Council of Europe, 2017: 7). Foregrounded in its 102-page inspection report was the warning to the MoJ that:

11 www.judiciary.gov.uk/wp-content/uploads/2017/03/Saunders-2017-0056.pdf.

12 www.judiciary.gov.uk/wp-content/uploads/2017/03/2017-0056-Response-by-NHS-England.pdf.

13 As the UK ratified the preventive, non-judicial European Convention for the Prevention of Torture and Inhuman or Degrading Treatment or Punishment in 1988, the European Committee for the Prevention of Torture and Inhuman or Degrading Treatment or Punishment is empowered to visit all places where persons are deprived of their liberty by a public authority. www.coe.int/en/web/conventions/full-list/-/conventions/treaty/126.

> unless determined action is taken to significantly reduce the current prison population, the regime improvements envisaged by the authorities' reform agenda will remain unattainable ... Over the last 25 years, the prison population has nearly doubled, and almost all adult prisons now operate at or near full operational capacity and well above their certified normal capacity. (Council of Europe, 2017: 8)

It is notable that the government is determinedly not (publicly) reducing the prison population, despite this clear warning from the Council of Europe, which was echoed by the Prison Governors Association.[14] The government response to the inspection focussed on investing in additional prison officers in public sector prisons (Council of Europe, 2018: 16–17).

Whilst oversight bodies are, by my assessment, producing vigorous and valuable critiques, the scope of their reporting and recommendations obfuscates pathways to improvement. I am especially concerned by the use of prison as a place of safety for people with severe mental illness (Pattinson, 2016). At HMP Woodhill, 'too many men who are accepted as needing to be transferred to hospital are subject to totally unacceptable delays. These delays are outside the control of the prison service and are consequence of a shortage of beds in secure hospitals and an under funding of mental health services in the community' (IMB, 2017: 5). Although mental health detention is not unproblematic, prisons are simply not equipped to manage or treat severe mental illness so it is morally and operationally pressing to stop using prisons as places of safety and expedite transfers to hospital. However, identifying imperatives or even

14 www.independent.co.uk/news/uk/home-news/uk-prison-population-conditions-government-urged-reduce-a7991351.html.

options for the future is challenging, amidst the hundreds of pages of reports produced every year.[15]

Post-suicide investigations are not the only detectors prisons are subject to. More generally, there are internal prison and Prison Service management processes and procedures (for example, for prisoner complaints), and private prisons are overseen by in-house Prison Service Controllers (Hood et al, 1999: 126). The Prison Act 1952 provides for a Chief Inspector of Prisons[16] (Section 5A), along with an IMB for each prison (Sections 6–9). Each prison in England and Wales is liable to be inspected at any time by its own IMB, which has 'a statutory right of free access to every part of the prison and to every prisoner at any time'[17] (Owen and Macdonald, 2015: 12). The Inspectorate now also operates 'an almost entirely unannounced inspection programme'.[18] Prisons will be inspected at least every five years, but most can expect to be inspected every two to three years. Prisons are also liable to inspection at any time by local authority Environmental Health Officers for food hygiene (Hood et al, 1999: 117) and HSE-appointed inspectors have the power to investigate reported injuries, dangerous occurrences and complaints (see Chapter Two). Every prison governor

[15] The adjourned Joint Committee on Human Rights Interim Report on Mental Health and Deaths in Prison (2017a: 8–9) recommended creating mechanisms to ensure the Secretary of State's accountability to Parliament for overcrowding and prison staffing levels, and also legal maximum times for transfer to secure hospital and time in cell.

[16] The current quasi-independent Prison Inspectorate was recommended by the 1979 May Committee Report, which was set up amidst the crisis of escalating industrial action by several branches of the Prison Officers' Association. Prior to this the Inspectorate was an internal Prison Service body which did not lay a report before Parliament (May 1979).

[17] Prison Act 1952, section 6(3), Prison Rules 1999, SI 1999/728, rr 74–80, Offender Management Act 2007, section 26.

[18] www.justiceinspectorates.gov.uk/hmiprisons/wp-content/uploads/sites/4/2014/02/1.-INSPECTION-FRAMEWORK-May-2017-1.pdf, p 11.

therefore needs to remember that tomorrow could be the day that one of these inspectorates arrives (Owers, 2010: 252).

In addition to these 'justice'-specific actors, further general actors oversee imprisonment, including the EHRC (statutory non-departmental body responsible for enforcing the Equality Act 2010, established by the Equality Act 2006[19]), the Treasury (the government's economic and finance ministry, which controls public spending[20]) and the NAO (which scrutinises public spending for Parliament and has statutory authority to examine whether departments have used their resources efficiently, effectively and with economy) (NAO, 2017: ii). Under the Government Resources and Accounts Act 2000, HMPPS (then NOMS) prepares a statement of accounts each financial year. These are certified by the NAO's Comptroller and Auditor General to the House of Commons. This process highlighted that NOMS breached HM Treasury guidelines and government pay policy three times in 2016–2017. NOMS responded to prison staffing shortfalls by temporarily increasing the rate of overtime and incident response pay by £5 per hour; adjusted the market supplements available to new prison officers in 31 sites with recruitment and retention difficulties *and* made additional payments to existing officers; and announced promotion opportunities for 2,000 officers in February 2017 without Treasury approval. In response, NOMS sought retrospective approval for these breaches, which HM Treasury denied. NOMS undertook an Internal Audit review, which identified failings in governance and made recommendations to improve governance, which HMPPS are implementing (NOMS, 2017: 68, 94). These three breaches led to approximately £8.8 million of payroll expenditure in excess of the approved pay remit and without appropriate authority, such that the Comptroller deemed these transactions irregular (NOMS, 2017: 94). This

19 www.equalityhumanrights.com/en/about-us/who-we-are.

20 www.gov.uk/government/organisations/hm-treasury/about.

is perhaps an indirect signal that NOMS had recognised the deleterious consequences of prison understaffing and attempted to respond, but was then sanctioned. The understaffing was however due to staff reductions ordered by former Secretary of State Chris Grayling (see Chapters One and Two) rather than NOMS.

The NAO also reported on mental health in prisons in 2017. It noted:

- 'NOMS' funding reduced by 13% between 2009–10 and 2016–17, and NOMS has reduced staff numbers in public prisons by 30% over the same period. Prisons have struggled to cope with reduced resources' (NAO, 2017: 8).
- 'NOMS does not monitor the quality of healthcare it pays for in the six privately managed prisons it oversees' (NAO, 2017: 7).
- 'NOMS and NHS England do not know how many prisoners are currently waiting to transfer to a secure hospital' (NAO, 2017: 9).
- 'The data on how many people in prison have mental health problems and how much government is spending to address this is poor. Consequently NOMS, NHS England and Public Health England do not know the base they are starting from, what they need to improve, or how realistic it is for them to meet their objectives. Without this understanding it is hard to see how government can be achieving value for money' (NAO, 2017: 11).

The NAO does not explain the stimulus for this report, but the EHRC's assertion is perhaps significant: 'Prisons need to monitor the numbers of prisoners with mental health conditions and their severity so that they can reflect on them and make appropriate arrangements for treatment and support' (EHRC, 2015a: 7). Although the NAO is a non-justice actor, the Comptroller and Auditor General only has powers to report to

Parliament,[21] which is equivalent to the effector power of the Inspectorate (HMIP, 2017: ii).

This section has demonstrated the range of prison detectors, including the post-death Ombudsman and Coroner investigations and, more generally, internal prison and Prison Service monitoring; private prison oversight by Controllers; potential prison inspections by the Inspectorate, IMB, Environmental Health Officers, Health and Safety Executive; systemic oversight by the European Committee for the Prevention of Torture, EHRC, Treasury and NAO. Although there are benefits associated with having multiple detectors from different sectors, this also constrains the remits of each overseer, deprioritises their recommendations, obfuscates valuable pathways to improvement (such as the need to stop criminalising the ill and expedite hospital transfers for prisoners with severe mental health problems) and constrains remedial action (as seen when prison staffing was increased in response to deteriorating conditions, contrary to Treasury guidelines). The next section examines effector mechanisms.

Prison effectors

Hood et al (1999: 137) characterised general prisons oversight in England and Wales as 'all bark, no bite', noting that 'the lack of powerful effectors to deploy against breach of standards created the risk of lack of credibility on the part of prisons regulators, even in their core information-gathering role'. Although I argue their bite is limited rather than absent, the Ombudsman, Coroner and the Inspectorate are not always seen by prison staff as lacking credibility (see also Chapter Three):

21 www.nao.org.uk/about-us/wp-content/uploads/sites/12/2016/10/The-Comptroller-and-Auditor-General-powers.pdf.

> Dave: 'a group of young prisoners, they said […] when the Inspectorate were coming they were trying so hard, for weeks and months, and they still got a fucking shite report!'

As explained in Chapter Two, the principal body that can give out sanctions to deter is the HSE in very specific circumstances. The CPS can prosecute prison staff but brings prosecutions extremely rarely. The MoJ can also fine *private* prison providers for breaches of contract[22] and their in-house Controllers wield 'a big stick' (Hood et al, 1999: 138). These effectors may contribute to the lower suicide rates in private prisons (van Ginneken et al, 2017) but equally private prisons have been characterised as providing more humane treatment to prisoners, better material prison conditions (such as newer buildings) and more time out of cell (Crewe et al, 2014). Other than these specific provisions, effectors following prison suicide are not entirely absent but they are weak, and generally limited to achieving improvements 'by persuading and shaming government' (Hood et al, 1999: 137) through producing publicly available reports.

Post-suicide Ombudsman reports and recommendations are not directly monitored but followed up by the Inspectorate as part of their general inspection programme. The Inspectorate's difficulties in effecting change are illustrated by the persistence of the Gurney wing at HMP Norwich. In August 2005 the Inspectorate found that parts of the prison were unfit for human habitation and recommended closure of a wing, which prison managers carried out (Owers, 2010: 252[23]). Overcrowding led to the wing being swiftly reopened, however. Prisoners then instructed lawyers, who requested an environmental health inspection, which the prison refused. It was not until a group of prisoners challenged that refusal through judicial review

---

22 www.theguardian.com/society/2016/apr/15/g4s-fined-100-times-since-2010-prison-contracts.

23 www.telegraph.co.uk/news/1540381/Unfit-prison-wing-reopened.html.

proceedings that the prison agreed to an environmental health inspection, which ultimately led to the wing's closure in October 2007.[24] Recipients of coroners' PFD reports must respond within 56 days but there is no further monitoring or assessment of the quality of the response. As noted in Chapter Two, there is potential to pursue responses from the Prisons Minister and the Secretary of State for Justice more vigorously and potential to monitor progress made in relation to PFD reports.

More generally, the principal means of effecting change in prisons is also the creation of reports and recommendations (for example, from the Inspectorate, Ombudsman, Council of Europe). The Inspectorate's annual report is presented to Parliament.[25] The Ombudsman's annual report is also presented to Parliament by the Secretary of State for Justice, by Command of her Majesty rather than statute. Follow-up mechanisms are very limited. The Inspectorate openly acknowledges this: 'as an independent inspectorate without formal powers, we rely upon persuasion, logic, goodwill and publicity to achieve our impact' (HMIP, 2017: 12). In the best-case scenario, systemic changes can be nudged forward through Inspectorate thematic reports, but these are slow-burners which take around a year to complete and 'even longer to influence practice and policy' (Owers, 2010: 253). Such hard-earned progress can also be quickly undone by changing political priorities, as illustrated in Chapter One.

I have argued that existing oversight mechanisms following prison suicide overly aim to persuade and shame individual prisons and staff members: government certainly deserves some more shaming and there is merit in directing succinct criticism to the government more directly (see Chapter Two). Systemic and policy criticism is a counterbalance to overseers'

[24] www.bindmans.com/news/prisoners-action-leads-to-closure-of-gurney-wing-hmp-norwich.

[25] Pursuant to section 5A of the Prison Act 1952 as amended by section 57 of the Criminal Justice Act 1982.

legitimising effect which can shore up prisons and their problematic practices (see Chapter One). The Inspectorate's novel Urgent Notification process, directed to the Secretary of State, may be a good mechanism to provide this direct input to government and could serve as an exemplar for other oversight bodies. But whilst an Urgent Notification is at least directed to decision-making level, it is still far from triggering a process of potentially escalating sanctions (if no action is taken) towards whole prisons being closed, for example, or private providers losing their licences to operate prisons.

Even in their current 'biteless' state without escalation or sanctioning abilities, oversight can have tangible effects. Nick Hardwick summarised the impact of his Inspectorate in 2016 as having stopped prison conditions deteriorating even further: 'In the adult estate, the reality is [that] things have got worse, and I think they would have been even worse were it not for us'.[26] For example, the 2017 inspection at HMP Liverpool led to a prisoner being moved to better conditions:

> 'I found a prisoner who had complex mental health needs being held in a cell that had no furniture other than a bed. The windows of both the cell and the toilet recess were broken, the light fitting in his toilet was broken with wires exposed, the lavatory was filthy and appeared to be blocked, his sink was leaking and the cell was dark and damp. Extraordinarily, this man had apparently been held in this condition for some weeks. The inspectors had brought this prisoner's circumstances to the attention of the prison, and it should not have needed my personal

[26] www.theguardian.com/society/2016/jan/29/prisons-inspector-nick-hardwick-interview.

> intervention for this man to be moved from such appalling conditions.'[27]

When retiring as Chief Inspector, Nick Hardwick told a related story from a young offender institution:

> He visited one institution and a boy asked him for help. 'I said, "What can I do?" and he said, "I want to go home to my Mummy", and echhhhh ...' He chokes up and can't complete his sentence. [...] 'I went on the warpath about the boy who wanted to go home to his Mummy, and got him into a hospital.'[28]

Furthermore, multiple Chief Inspectors have worked hard to improve prison conditions. Sir Stephen Tumin publicised impoverished regimes in insanitary prisons and produced an authoritative report in 1990 on prison suicide and self-harm (HMIP, 1990). Sir David Ramsbotham fiercely and publicly criticised prison conditions and produced a seminal report entitled *Suicide is Everyone's Concern*, which followed up Sir Tumin's work and concluded that 'the current strategy had only been partially implemented. There were serious deficiencies in the application of the policy' (HMIP, 1999: 3). His argument sadly endures.

Oversight creates a significant burden of investigation affecting prison staff, individual prisons, HMPPS and the MoJ. Whilst complex and overlapping regulatory formations can have advantages (Hood et al, 1999: 118), there are compliance costs associated with such an array of inspection and investigation bodies. To their credit, the Inspectorate works with other

27 www.justiceinspectorates.gov.uk/hmiprisons/wp-content/uploads/sites/4/2018/01/HMP-Liverpool-Web-2017.pdf, p 5.

28 www.theguardian.com/society/2016/jan/29/prisons-inspector-nick-hardwick-interview.

inspectorates to avoid multiple visits, partnering with, for example, HM Inspectorate of Constabulary, Ofsted, HM Inspectorate of Probation, the Care Quality Commission and the Royal Pharmaceutical Society.[29] Furthermore, Ombudsman reports use evidence from Inspectorate and IMB reports to substantiate their fatal incident report recommendations:

> More generally, the investigation has found evidence that Mr Giles had been taking new psychoactive substances (NPS) at Moorland and, at the time of his death, may have been in debt as a result. I share the concerns of the Chief Inspector and the Independent Monitoring Board that the prison needs to do more to reduce both supply and demand for NPS.[30]

> I also echo concerns raised by HMIP and the IMB about the need to more effectively safeguard the victims of bullying and investigate bullying. This is another matter I have raised with Bristol before.[31]

It is nevertheless questionable whether this burden is justified by the outcomes attained (see Chapter Three). This state of affairs is not attributable to lazy or ineffective regulators, but rather their inevitable limitations due to having 'no statutory powers to change the decisions of prison staff, still less to alter policy at a higher level' (Owen and Macdonald, 2015: 13).

29 www.justiceinspectorates.gov.uk/hmiprisons/wp-content/uploads/sites/4/2014/02/1.-INSPECTION-FRAMEWORK-May-2017-1.pdf, p 9.

30 https://s3-eu-west-2.amazonaws.com/ppo-prod-storage-1g9rkhjhkjmgw/uploads/2017/08/M007-16-Death-of-Mr-James-Giles-Moorland-Closed-06-04-2016-SID-22-30.pdf, p iii.

31 https://s3-eu-west-2.amazonaws.com/ppo-prod-storage-1g9rkhjhkjmgw/uploads/2017/07/L308-16-Death-of-Mr-Callum-Smith-Bristol-02-03-2016-SID-22-30.pdf, p iii.

Indeed, I suspect that oversight bodies have also been stretched by deteriorating prison conditions since 2012. They have not had the staff cuts experienced by prisons, but have not been resourced to meet increased demand for their services due to increasing prison deaths:

> Laura: 'It has probably *to date* protected us from cuts. We haven't had anything in the way of investment for a long time but we haven't been cut.'

My analysis is that prison overseers bark loudly, but overburden prison staff whereas government, specifically the Secretary of State and Ministers who have capacity to make systemic changes to prison regimes and imprisonment rates, certainly deserve persistent barks and probably some bites. Whilst existing prison overseers have limited bite, this should not dissuade them from barking at those who can effect systemic change. Oversight bodies could target government more succinctly, repeatedly and vigorously. If overseers do not do this, it absolves government of responsibility for prison conditions that are largely of their making and penalises prison staff for elements that are largely beyond their control. Given the legitimising effects of prisons oversight, overseers have a *responsibility* to speak truth to politicians, which (arguably) outweighs their remits. My position is that prisons overseers in England and Wales are currently functioning as more than legitimising functions that shore up state activity, but that they could achieve significantly more. However, this argument could be very different if my fieldwork had been undertaken at a time of less acute crisis in prisons. Change can also be effected through praising prison staff, and overseers could provide far more praise to prison staff,[32] seeking

32 Stretching the already overblown bite metaphor to suggest a lick is probably inappropriate.

to reinforce and spread examples of good practice, which is now considered.

Praise

Overseers most likely give praise during inspections and it is not entirely absent from reports. The 2017 inspection of HMP Downview found:

> One of its strengths was the high profile the governor and his senior management team maintained across the prison. Many women were positive about how visible, approachable and genuinely interested they were in helping them make positive changes to their lives. This was a fundamentally safe prison. Many indicators of safety, including the number of violent incidents, the frequency of use of force, the use of segregation and the number of adjudications were all lower than at other women's prisons. Fewer women than at other prisons also told us that they had felt unsafe there at some point. … Women said they felt safe on their first night. This was, possibly, testament to the supportive nature of relationships between staff and prisoners, which many prisoners spoke about throughout our inspection.[33]

Ombudsman reports have acknowledged good practice alongside deficiencies:

> Mr Roberts had severe anxiety and depression and a long history of intermittent suicidal thoughts. He received a significant amount of very good care at Glen Parva from the mental health service and the therapeutic drug and

33 www.justiceinspectorates.gov.uk/hmiprisons/wp-content/uploads/sites/4/2017/12/Downview-Web-2017.pdf, p 5.

> alcohol service. … Despite this good care, the investigation – with the benefit of hindsight – has identified some deficiencies in the way staff operated ACCT procedures from which the prison can learn.[34]

The EHRC praised HMP Gartree's Trigger Date Database, which lists wide-ranging trigger dates for prisoners who are or have been managed under ACCT procedures. The Safer Custody administrator collates information and feeds it to relevant departments prior to the date, with the offer of support such as a phone call to a family member. Gartree has found that this has reduced the number of ACCT documents being opened and has helped identify trends amongst the prison's repeated prolific self-harmers (EHRC, 2015a: 40–41). I am sceptical that trigger date databases are the silver bullet in prison suicide prevention, and wary that an overreliance on trigger dates could blind staff to dynamic risk factors. However, Gartree's initiative demonstrates a willingness to recognise and engage with prisoner problems, a recognition of prisoners as humans with emotions who are potentially in need of support, and an attempt to manage and solve problems in the institution, which are all helpful and valuable.

I therefore disagree that prisons inspectors are 'just hunting out deficiencies' (Seddon, 2010: 278), but amidst the very significant amounts of criticism from overseers, which prison staff feel the brunt of, there is a need for more praise and recognition. For example, the latest Inspectorate annual report stated:

> Despite pockets of good practice in suicide and self-harm prevention, prisoners in around a third of inspected establishments were negative about the overall care and

34 https://s3-eu-west-2.amazonaws.com/ppo-prod-storage-1g9rkhjhkjmgw/uploads/2017/07/M152-16-Death-of-Mr-Jamie-Roberts-Glen-Parva-12-08-2016-SID-22-30.pdf, p iii.

> support they received during their most vulnerable times. Staff shortages, increased violence and antisocial behaviour, widespread use of NPS and severely restricted regimes characterised many of the prisons we visited. … Around a third of the prisons inspected – including Leeds, Nottingham, Bedford, Winchester, Cardiff and Hewell – were not implementing or reinforcing PPO recommendations well enough, and they had all experienced further self-inflicted deaths since previous inspections. (HMIP, 2017: 21)

Clearly the numbers of self-inflicted deaths and levels of distress in the prison estate are entirely unacceptable and it is right that the Inspectorate challenges and publicises unacceptable conditions, triggered by Chris Grayling. But perhaps greater balance between the 'naming and shaming' and, for example, details of the 'pockets of good practice' would be useful, along with praising those working hard both on their own initiative and in response to regulator recommendations. A little detail of good practice is provided later in the report, but it does not make for enabling reading overall:

> Exeter made good use of a voluntary organisation, Choices Consultancy Service, with volunteers interviewing all new arrivals, assisting with family contact and providing practical information.[35] … Whatton had made efforts to address the experience and well-being of new arrivals. … The prison had undertaken a 'bus to bed' exercise in 2015 to understand and improve the experience for new arrivals, from their arrival in the escort van to location in their cell. The resulting action plan had improved outcomes for prisoners throughout the process. (HMCIP, 2017: 22)

35 This is swerving the issue that the state should adequately resource its prison receptions, but that debate is beyond the scope of this book.

There is also scope to give awards for good prison staff or teams, which might then provide something to aim for, recognition of good practice and learning that can be disseminated. Whilst such awards risk decorating justice: masking the injustices and painful nature of punishment behind claims of fairness, benevolence and care (Cheliotas, 2014), good staff morale is important for successful prisoner treatment (Liebling, 1992: 243). This might be challenging for the oversight community, which can struggle to find good practice:

> Laura: 'We also are supposed to identify good practice but honestly, because of the nature of our case work we are looking at something where there has almost always, and not always, but almost always been a failing.'

As Braithwaite and colleagues (2007: 320) note: 'finding a strength in the weakest of us … can be a base to build out new strengths that conquer our weaknesses. … There is no moral hazard in awarding prizes because they go to those who have laboured unusually hard to build their strength'. I therefore recommend that the Ombudsman and Inspectorate trial standalone 'good practice' documents, unsullied by criticisms. Prisons in their current condition are not entirely in control of the elements they must manage and are measured on so many areas that no investigation is devoid of weaknesses.

Prison oversight and prison suicide

Given the monstrous list of Prison Service Instructions and Orders, and the 500+ Expectations of the Inspectorate, it is important to note the 'paradox of reliability' found in a comparative study of nursing home oversight. In the Australian regime, 31 broad and vague inspection standards led to more reliable and consistent inspections and enabled inspectors to help develop better quality care than the US regime, based on over 1,000 detailed and precise rules. The Australian regime was able to be more resident-centred:

> the smaller the number of standards, the better the prospects of ensuring … that the most vital information for assessing the total quality of life and quality of care of residents is pursued … and … inspectors have the capacity to stand back to document the wider patterns in the problems they have identified. (Braithwaite and Braithwaite, 1995: 322)

Enabling prison staff and overseers to 'identify and diagnose problems and to focus on what actually matters most' could be beneficial (Seddon, 2010: 272) as prison staff cannot possibly have comprehensive knowledge of or the ability to implement all the Instructions and Orders, and could also lead to more productive investigations, such as from the Ombudsman.

For example, Mr Craig Royce hanged himself at HMP Chelmsford on 24 December 2016. The Ombudsman concluded that 'the overall care afforded to Mr Royce was not sufficient to keep him safe' (PPO, 2017d: i). Mr Royce had 'a long history of mental illness due to substance misuse and epilepsy' (PPO, 2017d: 1). Nevertheless, he 'had no meaningful contact with mental health or substance misuse services at Chelmsford' and 'was non-compliant with his epilepsy medication' (PPO, 2017d: 2). The Ombudsman recommendations about these issues were that the Governor and Head of Healthcare should ensure that:

- Prisoners with dual diagnosis receive appropriate integrated treatment.
- Mental health services meet the needs of prisoners at Chelmsford, with a referral system that results in face to face assessments using all relevant information for appropriate continuity of care and follow-up, and that prisoners have access to services equivalent to those in the community.

- Prisoners with epilepsy are accommodated and managed appropriately and that staff adhere to a protocol for epileptic prisoners in line with NICE guidelines (PPO, 2017d: 2).

Although this is an oversimplification of a complex case, it is possible that a practice guideline such as 'address prisoners' mental and physical health needs' could, potential prisoner stigmatisation notwithstanding, have led to prison staff realising that Mr Royce's mental and physical health problems were causing him difficulties and were not being addressed. Disguising this simple premise underneath 'protocol for epileptic prisoners' and 'dual diagnosis' and 'referral system' creates distance from and *depersonalises the human need and suffering* of Mr Royce. Creating and following a protocol for every eventuality of prison life does not encourage staff, policy makers and regulators to remember that prisoners are humans with physical and mental health needs. If we neglect these needs such that death results, it is hugely costly not only for the prisoner, their family and staff involved, but also for the general public.

There is, therefore, scope for the Prison Service and overseers to identify broad, subjective goals in order of priority. This would be a step change from existing practice but even within existing systems of overseers' concern about their remits and detailed assessment of staff implementation of procedures, clear critique of practices that are causing enormous harm is possible. Ideally this critique would be robustly directed to government as well as to prison staff when appropriate. Given the scope of published material pertaining to the state of prisons in England and Wales, the rest of us can also take up the campaigning baton.

I consider that Dean Saunders died because he was unsurprisingly *marooned* in prison. First, there was no other place of safety for him to go to from Basildon police station on

18 December 2015.[36] Then there was no mental health bed available for him on 21 December, when the prison psychiatrist assessed Mr Saunders as suitable for transfer to a secure hospital (PPO, 2016a). Next because prison healthcare staff missed an opportunity to transfer him to hospital on 31 December (apparently they believed that the prison psychiatrist needed to recommend this transfer but he was on leave). Mr Saunders electrocuted himself on 4 January 2016. Amidst forensic analysis of the specific circumstances and consideration of tweaks to operational policies (which will always be imperfectly implemented, albeit to greater and lesser extents), it is essential not to forget that this acutely unwell young father was marooned in prison, an inappropriate environment. We must recognise that he should not have gone to prison: very sick people need to go to hospital.

It might be reassuring to pretend that sick people becoming marooned in prison is a rare occurrence, attributable to policies that can and should be refined and reissued, but this is an unhelpful pretence. Like Dean, Sarah Reed became marooned in prison. She was remanded to HMP Holloway on 14 October 2015, solely for the purpose of obtaining reports on her fitness to plead and stand trial.[37] Despite being in prison for three months, the requisite two reports had not been obtained and no date for the hearing had been set when she died.[38] The Court ordered the reports on 27 October 2015 by emailing an administrative officer employed by the Central and North West London NHS Trust who worked from HMP Holloway. On 27 November 2015 this officer replied to the Court, apologised for the delay and indicated that the request should be redirected

[36] www.judiciary.gov.uk/wp-content/uploads/2017/03/Saunders-2017-0056.pdf.

[37] Section 4 Criminal Procedure (Insanity) Act 1964.

[38] www.judiciary.gov.uk/wp-content/uploads/2017/08/Sarah-Reed-2017-0208.pdf.

to the South London and Maudsley NHS Trust.[39] It is to be expected that internal prison administration will fail; indeed this book has provided example after example thereof. People die as a consequence.

There is truth in the argument that ombudsmen and coroners are partial agents of the state (Luce, 2007; Razack, 2015; Kendall, 2018). I agree that there are 'complex questions to be asked about the quality and purpose of all this official information, and the processes involved in its production' (Hancock and Liebling, 2013: 111). But *even these arguably compromised agents* identified that Dean Saunders and Sarah Reed *should not have been in prison.* In itself, this is a valuable contribution (see also Carver and Handley, 2016). It is perhaps, then, for the rest of us to take up the argument that the situations in which Dean Saunders and Sarah Reed died were not aberrations but foreseeable outcomes of marooning very sick people in prison, which continues to happen too commonly. 'We have seen time and again the links between mental illness, drug and alcohol dependencies, short sentences and potential for self-inflicted death. It must, therefore be seen that the imprisonment of such vulnerable people is at the root of the problem itself. … This incarceration is senseless' (Joint Committee on Human Rights, 2004: para 372). Who will be the next 'seriously unwell [person] being held in a prison setting which … [proves] incapable of keeping [them] safe?'[40] Who is 'barking' about this? Surely we all could?

---

[39] Ibid.

[40] https://s3-eu-west-2.amazonaws.com/ppo-prod-storage-1g9rkhjhkjmgw/uploads/2017/07/L250-16-Death-of-Ms-Sarah-Reed-Holloway-11-01-2016-SID-31-40.pdf.

References

Angiolini, E. (2017) *Report of the Independent Review of Deaths and Serious Incidents in Police Custody*. London: The Stationary Office (TSO).

Baker, D. V. (2016) *Deaths after Police Contact*. London: Palgrave Macmillan.

Barry, C. (2017) *Encountering Death in the Prison: An Exploration of Irish Prison Staff Experiences, Emotions and Engagements with Support*. Doctoral thesis, DIT (Dublin Institute of Technology), 2017.

Bartlett, A., Frater, A. and Hyde, S. (2018) 'Suicide and the criminal justice system: a more complete picture', *The Lancet Psychiatry*, *5*(2): 106-107.

Behan, C. and Kirkham, R. (2016) 'Monitoring, inspection and complaints adjudication in prison: the limits of prison accountability frameworks', *The Howard Journal of Crime and Justice*, *55*(4): 432-454.

Bell, D. (1999) 'Ethical issues in the prevention of suicide in prison', *Australian and New Zealand Journal of Psychiatry, 33*(5): 723-728.

Binswanger, I. A., Stern, M. F., Deyo, R. A., Heagerty, P. J., Cheadle, A., Elmore, J. G. and Koepsell, T. D. (2007) 'Release from prison - a high risk of death for former inmates', *New England Journal of Medicine*, *356*(2): 157-165.

Bollmann, M., Tidball-Binz, M., Elger, B. and Mangin, P. (2017) 'Investigation of deaths in custody', in Payne-James, J., Beynon, J. and Vieira, D. (Eds) *Monitoring Detention, Custody, Torture and Ill-treatment: A Practical Approach to Prevention and Documentation*. Boca Raton, FL: CRC Press, pp 231–248.

Braithwaite, J. and Braithwaite, V. (1995) 'The politics of legalism: rules versus standards in nursing-home regulation', *Social & Legal Studies*, *4*(3): 307-341.

Braithwaite, J., Makkai, T. and Braithwaite, V. A. (2007) *Regulating Aged Care: Ritualism and the New Pyramid*. Cheltenham: Edward Elgar.

Burton, F. and Carlen, P. (1979) *Official Discourse*. London: Routledge & Kegan Paul.

Calthorpe, B. and Choong, S. (2004) 'The coroner's court and the psychiatrist', *Advances in Psychiatric Treatment, 10*(2): 146-152.

Carroll, R., Hawton, K., Kapur, N., Bennewith, O. and Gunnell, D. (2012) 'Editor's choice: impact of the growing use of narrative verdicts by coroners on geographic variations in suicide: analysis of coroners' inquest data', *Journal of Public Health, 34*(3): 447-453.

Carver, R. (2016) 'United Kingdom', in Carver, R. and Handley, L. (Eds) *Does Torture Prevention Work?* Liverpool: Liverpool University Press, pp 105-142.

Carver, R. and Handley, L. (2016) 'Conclusion', in Carver, R. and Handley, L. (Eds) *Does Torture Prevention Work?* Liverpool: Liverpool University Press, pp 627-634.

Chamberlen, A. (2016) 'Embodying prison pain: women's experiences of self-injury in prison and the emotions of punishment', *Theoretical Criminology, 20*(2): 205-219.

Cheliotas (2014) 'Decorative justice: deconstructing the relationship between the arts and imprisonment', *International Journal for Crime, Justice and Social Democracy, 3*(1): 16-34.

Cliquennois, G. and Champetier, B. (2013) 'A new risk management for prisoners in France: the emergence of a death-avoidance approach', *Theoretical Criminology, 17*(3): 397-415.

Cole-King, A., Green, G., Gask, L., Hines, K. and Platt, S. (2013) 'Suicide mitigation: a compassionate approach to suicide prevention', *Advances in Psychiatric Treatment, 19*(4): 276-283.

Coles, D. and Shaw, H. (2012) *Learning from Death in Custody Inquests: A New Framework for Action and Accountability*. London: INQUEST.

Council of Europe (2017) *Report to the Government of the United Kingdom on the Visit to the United Kingdom carried out by the European Committee for the Prevention of Torture and Inhuman or Degrading Treatment or Punishment (CPT) from 30 March to 12 April 2016*. CPT/Inf (2017) 9.

Council of Europe (2018) *Response of the Government of the United Kingdom to the Report of the European Committee for the Prevention of Torture and Inhuman or Degrading Treatment or Punishment (CPT) on its Visit to the United Kingdom from 30 March to 12 April 2016.* CPT/Inf (2018) 1.

Coyle, A., Fair, H., Jacobson, J. and Walmsley, R. (2016) *Imprisonment Worldwide: The Current Situation and an Alternative Future.* Bristol: Policy Press.

Crewe, B. (2012) *The Prisoner Society: Power, Adaptation and Social Life in an English Prison.* Oxford: Oxford University Press.

Crewe, B., Liebling, A. and Hulley, S. (2014) 'Heavy–light, absent–present: rethinking the "weight" of imprisonment', *The British Journal of Sociology, 65*(3): 387-410.

Cross, C. and McArdle, I. (2016) 'Reports to prevent further deaths', in Cross, C. and Garnham, N. (Eds) *The Inquest Book: The Law of Coroners and Inquests.* Oxford: Hart, pp 503–516.

Doyle, J. M. (2010) 'Learning from error in American criminal justice', *The Journal of Criminal Law and Criminology, 100*(1): 109-148.

Doyle, D. and McGrath, J. (2016) 'Attributing criminal responsibility for workplace fatalities and deaths in custody : corporate manslaughter in Britain and Ireland', in Fitz-Gibbon, K. and Walklate, S. (Eds) *Homicide, Gender and Responsibility: An International Perspective*, Oxford: Routledge, pp 148-170.

Durkheim, E. (1952) *Suicide.* London: Routledge.

Dye, M. H. (2011) 'The gender paradox in prison suicide rates', *Women & Criminal Justice, 21*(4): 290-307.

Edelwich, J. and Brodsky, A. (1980) *Burn-out: Stages of Disillusionment in the Helping Professions.* New York: Human Sciences Press.

EHRC (2015a) *Preventing Deaths in Detention of Adults with Mental Health Conditions.* Available at: https://www.equalityhumanrights.com/sites/default/files/adult_deaths_in_detention_inquiry_report.pdf.

EHRC (2015b) *Inquiry into Non-natural Deaths in Detention of Adults with Mental Health Conditions, 2010–13. Evidence from the Families of those who have Died; Collected on Family Listening Day Event, 7 November 2014, Organised by INQUEST.* Available at: https://www.equalityhumanrights.com/sites/default/files/adult_deaths_in_detention_inquiry_family_listening_day_report.pdf.

Fazel, S., Ramesh, T. and Hawton, K. (2017) 'Suicide in prisons: an international study of prevalence and contributory factors', *The Lancet Psychiatry*, *4*(12): 946-952.

Field, S. and Jones, L. (2014) 'Are directors getting away with manslaughter? Emerging trends in prosecutions for corporate manslaughter', *Business Law Review*, *35*(5): 158-163.

Forrester, A., Exworthy, T., Olumoroti, O., Sessay, M., Parrott, J., Spencer, S. J. and Whyte, S. (2013) 'Variations in prison mental health services in England and Wales', *International Journal of Law and Psychiatry*, *36*(3-4): 326-332.

Forster, A. (2012). 'British judicial engagement and the juridification of the armed forces', *International Affairs*, *88*(2), 283–300.

Foster, S. (2005) 'The negligence of prison authorities and the protection of prisoner's rights', *Liverpool Law Review*, *26*(1): 75-99.

Fulwiler, C., Forbes, C., Santangelo, S. L. and Folstein, M. (1997) 'Self-mutilation and suicide attempt: distinguishing features in prisoners', *Journal of the American Academy of Psychiatry and the Law Online*, *25*(1): 69-77.

Gaggioli, G. and Elger, B. S. (2017) 'Death in custody: towards an international framework for investigation and prevention', in Elger, B. S., Ritter, C. and Stöver, H. (Eds) *Emerging Issues in Prison Health*. Dordrecht: Springer, pp 35-53.

Gilligan, G. and Pratt, J. (Eds) (2013) *Crime, Truth and Justice*. London: Routledge.

Girling, E. and Seal, L. (2016) 'Introduction: the deathscapes of incarceration', *Howard Journal of Crime and Justice*, *55*(3): 267–277.

Goffman E. (1963) *Stigma: Notes on the Management of Spoiled Identity*. Englewood Cliffs, NJ: Prentice Hall.

Goldson, B. and Coles, D. (2005) *In the Care of the State? Child Deaths in Penal Custody in England and Wales*. London: INQUEST.

Gooch, K. (2016) 'A childhood cut short: child deaths in penal custody and the pains of child imprisonment', *Howard Journal of Crime and Justice*, *55*(3): 278-294.

Gould, C., McGeorge, T. and Slade, K. (2017) 'Suicide screening tools for use in incarcerated offenders: a systematic review', *Archives of Suicide Research*, *22*(3): 345–364.

Griffin, S. and Moran, J. (2010) 'Accountability for deaths attributable to the gross negligent act or omission of a police force: the impact of the Corporate Manslaughter and Corporate Homicide Act 2007', *The Journal of Criminal Law*, *74*(4): 358-381.

Hancock, N. and Liebling, A. (2013) 'Truth, independence and effectiveness in prison inquiries', in Gilligan, G. and Pratt, J. (Eds) *Crime, Truth and Justice*. London: Routledge, pp 89-114.

Harbin, A. (2015) 'Prisons and palliative politics', in Adelsberg, G., Guenther, L. and Zeman, S. (Eds.) *Death and Other Penalties: Philosophy in a Time of Mass Incarceration*. New York: Fordham University Press, pp 158-173.

Harding, R. (2007) 'Inspecting prisons', in Jewkes, Y. (Ed) *Handbook on Prisons*. Cullompton: Willan, pp 534-565.

Harris, T. (2015) *Changing Prisons, Saving Lives: Report of the Independent Review into Self-inflicted Deaths in Custody of 18–24 Year Olds* (the Harris Review). London: TSO.

Henden, J. (2017) *Preventing Suicide: The Solution Focused Approach*. Hoboken, NJ: John Wiley & Sons.

HMIP (1990) *Report of a Review by Her Majesty's Chief Inspector of Prisons for England and Wales of Suicide and Self-harm in Prison Service Establishments in England and Wales.* Cm 1383. London: TSO.

HMIP (1995) *Report of HM Chief Inspector of Prisons for England and Wales. April 1994–March 1995*. London: TSO.

HMIP (1999) *Suicide is Everyone's Concern: A Thematic Review.* London: TSO.

HMIP (2017) *Annual Report 2016–17*. London: TSO.

Home Office (1994) *Report of the Enquiry into the Escape of Six Prisoners from the Special Security Unit at Whitemoor Prison, Cambridgeshire, on Friday 9th September 1994*. London: HMSO.

Hood, C., James, O., Scott, C., Jones, G. W. and Travers, T. (1999) *Regulation inside Government*. Oxford: Oxford University Press.

Hope, T. (2009) 'The illusion of control: a response to Professor Sherman', *Criminology & Criminal Justice*, *9*(2): 125-134.

House of Commons (2006) *Report of the Zahid Mubarek Inquiry*. HC 1082-1.

House of Commons (2013) *Report of the Mid Staffordshire NHS Foundation Trust Public Inquiry: Executive Summary*. HC 947.

House of Commons (2017) *Government Responses to the Committee's Reports of Session 2016–17 on: Prison Reform: Governor Empowerment and Prison Performance*. HC 491.

Howard League (2016a) *The Cost of Prison Suicide: Research Briefing*. London: Howard League.

Howard League (2016b) *Preventing Prison Suicide: Perspectives from the Inside*. London: Howard League.

IMB (2015) *Independent Monitoring Board HMP Woodhill Annual Report 2015 (1 June 2014–31 May 2015)*. https://s3-eu-west-2.amazonaws.com/imb-prod-storage-1ocod6bqky0vo/uploads/2015/09/Woodhill-2014-15.pdf.

IMB (2016) *Independent Monitoring Board HMP Woodhill Annual Report 2016 (1 June 2015–31 May 2016)*. https://s3-eu-west-2.amazonaws.com/imb-prod-storage-1ocod6bqky0vo/uploads/2016/10/Woodhill-2015-16.pdf.

IMB (2017) *Annual Report of the Independent Monitoring Board at HMP Woodhill (1 June 2016–30 May 2017)*, November 2017. https://s3-eu-west-2.amazonaws.com/imb-prod-storage-1ocod6bqky0vo/uploads/2017/11/Woodhill-2016-17.pdf.

Joint Committee on Human Rights (2004) *Third Report*. London: TSO.

Joint Committee on Human Rights (2017a) *Mental Health and Deaths in Prison: Interim Report*. London: TSO.

Joint Committee on Human Rights (2017b) *Uncorrected Oral Evidence: Mental Health and Deaths in Prison*. http://data.parliament.uk/writtenevidence/committeeevidence.svc/evidencedocument/human-rights-committee/mental-health-and-deaths-in-prison/oral/47921.html.

Jordan, J. T. and Samuelson, K. W. (2015) 'Predicting suicide intent: the roles of experiencing or committing violent acts', *Suicide and Life-Threatening Behavior*, *46*(3): 293-300.

Kendall, J. (2018) *Regulating Police Detention: Voices from Behind Closed Doors*. Bristol: Policy Press.

Kottler, C., Smith, J. G. and Bartlett, A. (2018) 'Patterns of violence and self-harm in women prisoners: characteristics, co-incidence and clinical significance', *The Journal of Forensic Psychiatry & Psychology*. www.tandfonline.com/doi/abs/10.1080/14789949.2018.1425475.

Lageson, S. E. and Maruna, S. (2018) 'Digital degradation: stigma management in the internet age', *Punishment & Society*, *20*(1): 113-133.

Lamb, H. R., Weinberger, L. E. and DeCuir Jr, W. J. (2002) 'The police and mental health', *Psychiatric Services*, *53*(10): 1266-1271.

Lancaster, D (2001) 'Suicide and self-harm among women and girls in HMP Holloway', *Prison Service Journal*, *138*: 19–21.

Lappi-Seppälä, T. and Koskenniemi, L. (2017) 'National and regional instruments in securing the rule of law and human rights in the Nordic prisons', *Crime, Law and Social Change*, https://link.springer.com/content/pdf/10.1007/s10611-017-9723-1.pdf.

Larney, S. and Farrell, M. (2017) 'Prisoner suicide: a multilevel problem', *The Lancet Psychiatry*, *4*(12): 894-895.

Laxminarayan, M. (2013) 'Interactional justice, coping and the legal system: needs of vulnerable victims', *International Review of Victimology*, *19*(2): 145-158.

Lazarus, L. (2004) *Contrasting Prisoners' Rights: A Comparative Examination of Germany and England*. Oxford: Oxford University Press.

Leach, P. (2011) *Report on the IAP's Work Stream Considering Investigations of Deaths in Custody – Compliance with Article 2 ECHR*. http://iapdeathsincustody.independent.gov.uk/wp-content/uploads/2012/01/IAP-Workstream-Paper-on-Article-2-Compliant-Investigations.pdf.

Leese, M., Thomas, S. and Snow, L. (2006) 'An ecological study of factors associated with rates of self-inflicted death in prisons in England and Wales', *International Journal of Law and Psychiatry*, *29*(5): 355-360.

Liebling, A. (1992) *Suicides in Prison*. Abingdon: Routledge.

Liebling, A. (1998) 'Managing to prevent prison suicide', in Kamerman, J. B. (Ed) *Negotiating Responsibility in the Criminal Justice System*. Carbondale, IL: SIU Press, pp 68-86.

Liebling, A. (2007) 'Prison suicide and its prevention', in Jewkes, Y. (Ed) *Handbook on Prisons*. Cullompton: Willan, pp 423-446.

Liebling, A. and Ludlow, A. (2016) 'Suicide, distress and the quality of prison life', in Jewkes, Y., Crewe, B. and Bennett, J. (Eds) *Handbook on Prisons*. London: Routledge, pp 224-245.

Liebling, A., Price, D. and Shefer, G. (2010) *The Prison Officer*. Abingdon: Routledge.

Livingstone, S., Owen, T., Macdonald, A., Ghrálaigh, B. N. and Law, H. (2008) *Prison Law*. Oxford: Oxford University Press.

Luce, T. (2007) 'Reform of the coroner system and death certification', *BMJ: British Medical Journal*, *335*(7622): 680-681.

Ludlow, A., Schmidt, B., Akoensi, T., Liebling, A., Giacomantonio, C. and Sutherland, A. (2015) *Self-inflicted Deaths in NOMS' Custody amongst 18–24 Year Olds*. Cambridge: RAND Europe.

Madsen, P., Dillon, R. L. and Tinsley, C. H (2016) 'Airline safety improvement through experience with near☒misses: a cautionary tale', *Risk Analysis*, *36*(5): 1054-1066.

Maganty, D., Tovey, M., Routhu, S., Aslam, A. (2015) *The Harris Review: Analysis of the Clinical Reviews (with inclusion of case summary data)*. http://iapdeathsincustody.independent.gov.uk/harris-review/harris-review-research-2./.

Marzano, L., Ciclitira, K. and Adler, J. (2012) 'The impact of prison staff responses on self-harming behaviours: prisoners' perspectives', *British Journal of Clinical Psychology*, *51*(1): 4-18.

May, J. D. (1979) *Committee of Inquiry into the United Kingdom Prison Services, Report*. Cm 7673. London: TSO.

McArdle, I. (2016) 'The role and scope of an inquest', in Cross, C. and Garnham, N. (Eds) *The Inquest Book: The Law of Coroners and Inquests*. Oxford: Hart, pp 39–54.

McKenzie, J (2014) *Submission to the Harris Review*. http://iapdeathsincustody.independent.gov.uk/wp-content/uploads/2015/08/Jane-MacKenzie.pdf.

McKinnon, I. and Finch, T. (2018) 'Contextualising health screening risk assessments in police custody suites – qualitative evaluation from the HELP-PC study in London, UK', *BMC Public Health*, *18*(1): 393.

Meade, B., Steiner, B. and Klahm IV, C. F. (2017) 'The effect of police use of force on mental health problems of prisoners', *Policing and Society*, *27*(2): 229-244.

Mendas (2012) *Deaths in Custody: The Impact of Coroners' Rule 43 Reports on Organisational Learning*. London: Mendas Ltd.

Mills, R. W. and Reiss, D. R. (2014) 'Secondary learning and the unintended benefits of collaborative mechanisms: the Federal Aviation Administration's voluntary disclosure programs', *Regulation & Governance*, *8*(4): 437-454.

MoJ (2013) PS1 64/2011 *Management of Prisoners at Risk of Harm to Self, to Others and From Others (Safer Custody)*. Available at: https://www.justice.gov.uk/offenders/psis/prison-service-instructions-2011

MoJ (2014) *Safety in Custody Statistics England and Wales: Update to March 2014*. London: TSO.

MoJ (2016) *Prison Safety and Reform*. London: TSO.

MoJ (2017) *Safety in Custody Statistics Bulletin, England and Wales, Deaths in Prison Custody to December 2016 Assaults and Self-Harm to September 2016*. London: TSO.

MoJ (2018) *Safety in Custody Statistics Bulletin, England and Wales, Deaths in Prison Custody to December 2017 Assaults and Self-harm to September 2017*. London: TSO.

Mowbray, A (2002) 'Duties of investigation under the European Convention on Human Rights', *International & Comparative Law Quarterly*, *51*(2): 437–448.

NAO (2017) *Her Majesty's Prison & Probation Service, NHS England and Public Health England: Mental Health in Prisons*. HC 42. London: TSO.

NOMS (2017) *National Offender Management Service Annual Report and Accounts 2016–2017*. HC 198. London: TSO.

NPCC/PPO (2015) *Memorandum of Understanding between the National Police Chiefs' Council and the Prisons and Probation Ombudsman*. https://s3-eu-west-2.amazonaws.com/ppo-prod-storage-1g9rkhjhkjmgw/uploads/2015/07/MoU_PPO_NPCC-FINAL-2015.pdf.

Owen, T. and Macdonald, A. (Ed) (2015) *Livingstone, Owen, and Macdonald on Prison Law* (5th edn). Oxford: Oxford University Press.

Owers, A. (2010) 'The regulation of criminal justice: inspectorates, ombudsmen and inquiries', in Quirk, H., Seddon, T. and Smith, G. (Eds.) *Regulation and Criminal Justice: Innovations in Policy and Research*. Cambridge: Cambridge University Press, pp 237–260.

Parsloe, P. (1976) 'Social work and the justice model', *British Journal of Social Work*, *6*(1): 71–89.

Pattinson, T. (2016) *Prison as a Place of Safety for Women with Complex Health Needs*. London: Griffins Society.

Paul, J. L., Neufeld, G. R. and Pelossi, J. W. (1977) *Child Advocacy within the System*. Syracuse, NY: Syracuse University Press.

Peay, J. (1996) 'Themes and questions: the inquiry in context', in Peay, J. (Ed) *Inquiries after Homicide*. London: Duckworth, pp 9–38.

Phillips, J., Gelsthorpe, L. and Padfield, N. (2017) 'Non-custodial deaths: missing, ignored or unimportant?', *Criminology & Criminal Justice*. http://journals.sagepub.com/doi/abs/10.1177/1748895817745939.

Powell, J., Geddes, J., Hawton, K., Deeks, J. and Goldcacre, M. (2000) 'Suicide in psychiatric hospital in-patients: risk factors and their predictive power', *The British Journal of Psychiatry*, *176*(3): 266–272.

PPO (2014a) *Investigation into the Death of a Man in January 2014 at HMP Winchester*. A Report by the Prisons and Probation Ombudsman Nigel Newcomen CBE, July 2014. www.ppo.gov.uk/app/uploads/2015/09/J002-14-Death-of-a-male-prisoner-Winchester-03-01-2014-SID-22-30.pdf.

PPO (2014b) *Clinical Review following a Death in Custody Investigated by the Prisons and Probation Ombudsman. Part 2 – Guidance for Clinical Reviewers. Updated September 2014*. www.ppo.gov.uk/app/uploads/2014/07/PPO-Clinical-Reviews-Part-2-Guidance-clinical-reviewers-September-2014.pdf.

PPO (2015a) *Investigation into the Death of a Man at HMP Liverpool in April 2014*. A Report by the Prisons and Probation Ombudsman Nigel Newcomen CBE, January 2015. https://s3-eu-west-2.amazonaws.com/ppo-prod-storage-1g9rkhjhkjmgw/uploads/2016/05/K010-14-death-of-a-male-prisoner-Liverpool-Self-Inflicted-14-04-2014-51-60.pdf.

PPO (2015b) *Investigation into the Death of a Man at HMP Haverigg in May 2014*. A Report by the Prisons and Probation Ombudsman Nigel Newcomen CBE, February 2015. https://s3-eu-west-2.amazonaws.com/ppo-prod-storage-1g9rkhjhkjmgw/uploads/2015/11/K022-14-Death-of-a-male-prisoner-in-hospital-Haverigg-09-05-2014-SID-22-30.pdf.

PPO (2015c) *Independent Investigation Report by the Prisons and Probation Ombudsman Nigel Newcomen CBE into the Death of a Man, a Prisoner at HMP Pentonville, in December 2014, August 2015*. https://s3-eu-west-2.amazonaws.com/ppo-prod-storage-1g9rkhjhkjmgw/uploads/2015/11/K183-14-Death-of-a-male-prisoner-in-hospital-Pentonville-09-12-2014-SID-31-40.pdf.

PPO (2015d) *Independent Investigation into the Death of a Prisoner at HMP Woodhill in February 2015.* A Report by the Prisons and Probation Ombudsman Nigel Newcomen CBE, November 2015. https://s3-eu-west-2.amazonaws.com/ppo-prod-storage-1g9rkhjhkjmgw/uploads/2016/01/K236-15-Death-of-a-male-prisoner-in-hospital-Woodhill-27-02-2015-SID-22-30.pdf.

PPO (2016a) *Independent Investigation into the Death of Mr Dean Saunders a Prisoner at HMP Chelmsford on 4 January 2016.* A Report by the Prisons and Probation Ombudsman Nigel Newcomen CBE, September 2016. https://s3-eu-west-2.amazonaws.com/ppo-prod-storage-1g9rkhjhkjmgw/uploads/2017/01/L246-16-Death-of-Mr-Dean-Saunders-Chelmsford-04-01-2016-SID-22-30.pdf.

PPO (2016b) *Independent Investigation into the Death of Mr Simon Turvey a Prisoner at HMP Woodhill on 29 December 2015.* A Report by the Prisons and Probation Ombudsman Nigel Newcomen CBE, September 2016. https://s3-eu-west-2.amazonaws.com/ppo-prod-storage-1g9rkhjhkjmgw/uploads/2017/01/L236-15-Death-of-Mr-Simon-Turvey-Woodhill-29-12-2015-SID-22-30.pdf.

PPO (2016c) *Independent Investigation into the Death of Mr Ireneusz Polubinski a Prisoner at HMP Woodhill on 31 January 2016.* A Report by the Prisons and Probation Ombudsman Nigel Newcomen CBE, September 2016. https://s3-eu-west-2.amazonaws.com/ppo-prod-storage-1g9rkhjhkjmgw/uploads/2017/02/L273-16-Death-of-Mr-Ireneusz-Polubinski-HMP-Woodhill-31-01-2016-SID-51-60.pdf.

PPO (2017a) *Annual Report 2016–2017.* www.ppo.gov.uk/document/annual-reports/.

PPO (2017b) *Independent Investigation into the Death of Mr Daniel Dunkley a Prisoner at HMP Woodhill on 2 August 2016.* A Report by the Prisons and Probation Ombudsman Nigel Newcomen CBE, April 2017. https://s3-eu-west-2.amazonaws.com/ppo-prod-storage-1g9rkhjhkjmgw/uploads/2017/05/M139-16-Death-of-Mr-Daniel-Dunkley-in-hospital-Woodhill-02-08-2016-SID-31-40.pdf.

PPO (2017c) *Independent Investigation into the Death of Mr Thomas Morris a Prisoner at HMP Woodhill on 26 June 2016*. A Report by the Prisons and Probation Ombudsman Nigel Newcomen CBE, June 2017. https://s3-eu-west-2.amazonaws.com/ppo-prod-storage-1g9rkhjhkjmgw/uploads/2017/09/M103-16-Death-of-Mr-Thomas-Morris-Woodhill-26-06-2016-SID-31-40.pdf.

PPO (2017d) *Independent Investigation into the Death of Mr Craig Royce a Prisoner at HMP Chelmsford on 25 December 2016*. A Report by the Prisons and Probation Ombudsman Nigel Newcomen CBE, October 2017. https://s3-eu-west-2.amazonaws.com/ppo-prod-storage-1g9rkhjhkjmgw/uploads/2018/01/M291-16-Death-of-Mr-Craig-Royce-Chelmsford-SID-25-12-2016-41-50.pdf.

PPO/CSEW (2012) *Memorandum of Understanding between the Prisons and Probation Ombudsman (PPO) and the Coroners Society of England and Wales (CSEW)*. https://s3-eu-west-2.amazonaws.com/ppo-prod-storage-1g9rkhjhkjmgw/uploads/2014/07/Memorandum_of_Understanding_with_Coroners_-_approved_July_2012.pdf.

Pratt, J. and Eriksson, A. (2013) *Contrasts in Punishment: An Explanation of Anglophone excess and Nordic exceptionalism*. London: Routledge.

Pridmore, S. and Pridmore, W. (2017) 'The conundrum of hanging points in correctional facilities', *Australasian Psychiatry*, *25*(1): 40–42.

Prison Reform Trust (2017) *Prison: The Facts. Bromley Briefings Summer 2017*. www.prisonreformtrust.org.uk/Portals/0/Documents/Bromley%20Briefings/Summer%202017%20factfile.pdf.

Procter, N. G., De Leo, D. and Newman, L. (2013) 'Suicide and self-harm prevention for people in immigration detention', *Medical Journal of Australia*, *199*: 730–732.

Razack, S. (2015) *Dying from Improvement: Inquests and Inquiries into Indigenous Deaths in Custody*. Toronto: University of Toronto Press.

Resodihardjo, S. (2009) *Crisis and Change in the British and Dutch Prison Services: Understanding Crisis-reform Processes*. Abingdon: Routledge.

Richards, J. (2007) *What is Required to Satisfy the Investigative Obligation under Article 2 and/or 3 ECHR?* Report: 39 Essex Street. www.39essex.com/docs/articles/JR_Article2&3_seminar_250107.pdf.

Rivlin, A., Hawton, K., Marzano, L. and Fazel, S. (2013) 'Psychosocial characteristics and social networks of suicidal prisoners: towards a model of suicidal behaviour in detention', *PloS one*, *8*(7): e68944.

Rowe, A. (2011) 'Narratives of self and identity in women's prisons: stigma and the struggle for self-definition in penal regimes', *Punishment & Society*, *13*(5): 571-591.

Rutherford, H. and Taylor, P. J. (2004) 'The transfer of women offenders with mental disorder from prison to hospital', *Journal of Forensic Psychiatry & Psychology*, *15*(1): 108-123.

Scott Bray, R. (2017) 'Death investigation and human rights', in Weber, L., Fishwick, E. and Marmo, M. (Eds) *The Routledge International Handbook of Criminology and Human Rights*. Abingdon: Routledge.

Scraton, P. and Chadwick, K. (1986) 'Speaking ill of the dead: institutionalised responses to deaths in custody', *Journal of Law and Society*, *13*(1): 93-115.

Seddon, T. (2010) 'Rethinking prison inspection: regulating institutions of confinement', in Quirk, H., Seddon, T. and Smith, G. (Eds) *Regulation and Criminal Justice: Innovations in Policy and Research*. Cambridge: Cambridge University Press, pp 261-282.

Seneviratne, M. (2010) 'The prisons and probation ombudsman: a review', *Nottingham Law Journal*, *19*(2): 1–21.

Shapland, J., Willmore, J. and Duff, P. (1985) *Victims in the Criminal Justice System*. Aldershot: Gower.

Shaw, S. (2005) *Inquiry into Allegations of Racism and Mistreatment of Detainees at Oakington Immigration Reception Centre and while under Escort*. London: Prisons and Probation Ombudsman for England and Wales.

Shaw, S. (2017) *Independent Professional Advice on the Prevention of Self-Inflicted Deaths and Self-Harm at HMP Woodhill*. http://iapdeathsincustody.independent.gov.uk/wp-content/uploads/2018/02/Advice-on-self-inflicted-deaths-and-self-harm-at-HMP-Woodhill-Stephen-Shaw.pdf.

Shaw, H. and Coles, D. (2007) *Unlocking the Truth: Families' Experiences of the Investigation of Deaths in Custody*. London: INQUEST.

Skelton, P. and Williams, L. (2016) 'Deaths in custody', in Cross, C. and Garnham, N. (Eds) *The Inquest Book: The Law of Coroners and Inquests*. Oxford: Hart, pp 405–428.

Skelton, P., Cross, C. and Beattie, K. (2016) 'Article 2 inquests', in Cross, C. and Garnham, N. (Eds) *The Inquest Book: The Law of Coroners and Inquests*. Oxford: Hart, pp 77–136.

Slade, K. (2018) 'Dual harm: an exploration of the presence and characteristics for dual violence and self-harm behaviour in prison', *Journal of Criminal Psychology*, *8*(2): 97-111.

Smith, G. (2010) 'Every complaint matters: Human Rights Commissioner's opinion concerning independent and effective determination of complaints against the police', *International Journal of Law, Crime and Justice*, *38*(2): 59-74.

Smith, A. R., Witte, T. K., Teale, N. E., King, S. L., Bender, T. W. and Joiner, T. E. (2008) 'Revisiting impulsivity in suicide: implications for civil liability of third parties', *Behavioral Sciences & the Law*, *26*(6): 779-797.

South, C. R. and Wood, J. (2006) 'Bullying in prisons: the importance of perceived social status, prisonization, and moral disengagement', *Aggressive Behavior*, *32*(5): 490-501.

Stern, V. (2010) 'The role of citizens and non-profit advocacy organizations in providing oversight', *Pace Law Review*, *30*(5): 1529-1534.

Steinerte, E. (2014) 'The jewel in the crown and its three guardians: independence of national preventive mechanisms under the Optional Protocol to the UN Torture Convention', *Human Rights Law Review*, *14*(1): 1-29.

Steinerte, E. and Murray, R. (2009) 'Same but different? National human rights commissions and ombudsman institutions as national preventive mechanisms under the Optional Protocol to the UN Convention against Torture', *Essex Human Rights Review*, *6*(1): 54–72.

Stirton, L. and Lodge, M. (2001) 'Transparency mechanisms: building publicness into public services', *Journal of Law and Society*, *28*(4): 471-489.

Stoliker, B. E. (2018) 'Attempted suicide: a multilevel examination of inmate characteristics and prison context', *Criminal Justice and Behavior*, *45*(5): 589-611.

Sweeney, F., Clarbour, J. and Oliver, A. (2018) 'Prison officers' experiences of working with adult male offenders who engage in suicide-related behaviour', *The Journal of Forensic Psychiatry & Psychology*, *29*(3): 467-482.

Tait, G., Carpenter, B., De Leo, D. and Tatz, C. (2015) 'Problems with the coronial determination of "suicide"', *Mortality*, *20*(3): 233-247.

Thoonen, E. C. M. (2017) *Death in State Custody: Obligations to Prevent Premature Death of Detainees and to Investigate Deaths of Detainees pursuant to the European Convention on Human Rights*. Antwerp: Maklu.

Towl, G. and Crighton, D. (2017) *Suicide in Prisons: Prisoners' Lives Matter*. Hook: Waterside Press.

Van Ginneken, E. F., Sutherland, A. and Molleman, T. (2017) 'An ecological analysis of prison overcrowding and suicide rates in England and Wales, 2000–2014', *International Journal of Law and Psychiatry*, *50*: 76-82.

Van Zyl Smit, D. (2010) 'Regulation of prison conditions', *Crime and Justice*, *39*(1): 503-563.

Wacquant, L. (2009) *Punishing the Poor: The Neoliberal Government of Social Insecurity*. London: Duke University Press.

Walker, T. and Towl, G. (2016) *Preventing Self-injury and Suicide in Women's Prisons*. London: Waterside Press.

Walker, T., Shaw, J., Hamilton, L., Turpin, C., Reid, C. and Abel, K. (2017) '"Coping with the job": prison staff responding to self-harm in three English female prisons: a qualitative study', *The Journal of Forensic Psychiatry & Psychology*, *28*(6): 811-824.

Wangmo, T., Ruiz, G., Sinclair, J., Mangin, P. and Elger, B. S. (2014) 'The investigation of deaths in custody: a qualitative analysis of problems and prospects', *Journal of Forensic and Legal Medicine*, *25*: 30-37.

Wheeler, M. (2016) 'The Coroner', in Cross, C. and Garnham, N. (Eds) *The Inquest Book: The Law of Coroners and Inquests*. Oxford: Hart, pp 55–68.

Whittall, E. (2017) 'A judicial review to compel HMP Woodhill to comply with national prison standards on preventing self-inflicted deaths was a missed opportunity to advance the law', *INQUEST Law July 2017*: 3-4.

Wright, N., Tompkins, C. N. E. and Mohammed, Z. (2012) 'Cross examination of clinicians at coroners' inquests following deaths in custody', *International Journal of Prisoner Health, 8*(3): 92-98.

World Health Organization (2007) *Preventing Suicide in Jails and Prisons*. Geneva: World Health Organization. www.who.int/iris/handle/10665/43678.

Yalom, I. D. (2017) *Becoming Myself*. New York: Basic Books.

Zedner, L. (2004) *Criminal Justice*. Oxford: Oxford University Press.

Index

References to figures and tables are in *italics*. References to notes are the page number followed by '*n*' then the note number (eg. 56*n*39)